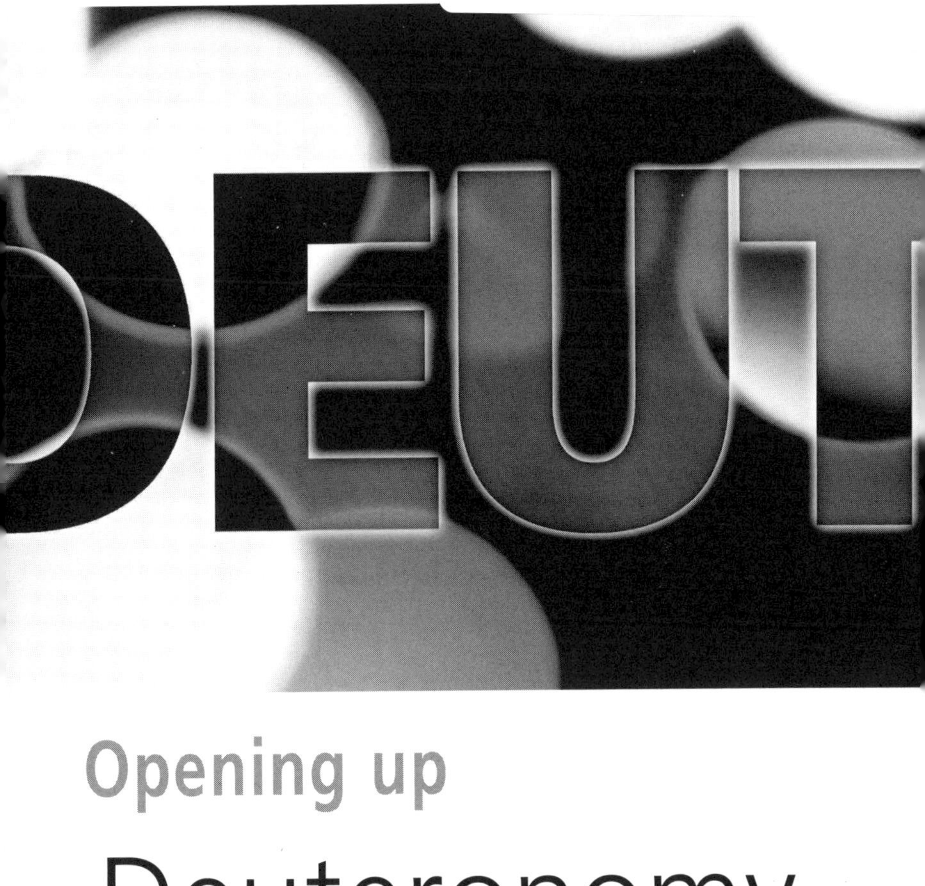

Opening up
Deuteronomy

ANDREW THOMSON

This commentary captures so well the message of Deuteronomy. It appreciates the significance of the book as a covenant renewal document, and is perceptive in its comments, lively in style and most helpful in relating the teaching of the book to the overall theology of the Bible. Bible students and preachers will find it stimulating, and it will help them grasp Deuteronomy's overall structure and teaching. I will be recommending it warmly; I know that readers will find that it opens up a fresh understanding of Deuteronomy that can be fruitfully conveyed to others.

Allan M. Harman, former Principal and Professor of Old Testament, Presbyterian Theological College, Melbourne, Australia, and author of *Deuteronomy: The Commands of a Covenant God* (Christian Focus, 2001).

Crisp, clear and contemporary. The whole of Deuteronomy is explained as an exposition of the Ten Commandments in a way that makes this three-and-a-half-thousand-year-old book relevant for the twenty-first century. The study and discussion questions at the close of each chapter extend its value well beyond this little volume. For any who wish to delve into Deuteronomy either as a group or for private study, this is just right.

Brian Edwards, Christian minister, author and editor

© Day One Publications 2015

First printed 2015

All Scripture quotations, unless stated otherwise, are from the anglicized edition of the ESV Bible copyright © 2002 Collins, part of HarperCollins Publishers.

All rights reserved.

ISBN 978-1-84625-483-3

British Library Cataloguing in Publication Data available
Published by Day One Publications
Ryelands Road, Leominster, England, HR6 8NZ
Telephone 01568 613 740 FAX 01568 611 473
email—sales@dayone.co.uk
web site—www.dayone.co.uk

All rights reserved
No part of this publication may be reproduced, or stored in a retrieval system, or transmitted, in any form or by any means, mechanical, electronic, photocopying, recording or otherwise, without the prior permission of Day One Publications.
Printed by TJ International

Dedication
To our children,
Esther, Gemma and Joel,
to whom I often seem to be 'laying down the law', but with the same heart of love as the Lawgiver in Deuteronomy!

List of Bible abbreviations

THE OLD TESTAMENT		1 Chr.	1 Chronicles	Dan.	Daniel
		2 Chr.	2 Chronicles	Hosea	Hosea
Gen.	Genesis	Ezra	Ezra	Joel	Joel
Exod.	Exodus	Neh.	Nehemiah	Amos	Amos
Lev.	Leviticus	Esth.	Esther	Obad.	Obadiah
Num.	Numbers	Job	Job	Jonah	Jonah
Deut.	Deuteronomy	Ps.	Psalms	Micah	Micah
Josh.	Joshua	Prov.	Proverbs	Nahum	Nahum
Judg.	Judges	Eccles.	Ecclesiastes	Hab.	Habakkuk
Ruth	Ruth	S.of S.	Song of Solomon	Zeph.	Zephaniah
1 Sam.	1 Samuel	Isa.	Isaiah	Hag.	Haggai
2 Sam.	2 Samuel	Jer.	Jeremiah	Zech.	Zechariah
1 Kings	1 Kings	Lam.	Lamentations	Mal.	Malachi
2 Kings	2 Kings	Ezek.	Ezekiel		

THE NEW TESTAMENT		Gal.	Galatians	Heb.	Hebrews
		Eph.	Ephesians	James	James
Matt.	Matthew	Phil.	Philippians	1 Peter	1 Peter
Mark	Mark	Col.	Colossians	2 Peter	2 Peter
Luke	Luke	1 Thes.	1 Thessalonians	1 John	1 John
John	John	2 Thes.	2 Thessalonians	2 John	2 John
Acts	Acts	1 Tim.	1 Timothy	3 John	3 John
Rom.	Romans	2 Tim.	2 Timothy	Jude	Jude
1 Cor.	1 Corinthians	Titus	Titus	Rev.	Revelation
2 Cor.	2 Corinthians	Philem.	Philemon		

Contents

	Background and summary	9
	Part 1 The review	19
❶	The rebellion (1:1–46)	20
❷	The wilderness (2:1–3:29)	29
❸	The warning (4:1–43)	38
	Part 2 The rules	47
❹	The law (4:44–6:25)	48
❺	Commandment one: the devotion principle (7:1–11:32)	58
❻	Commandments two to four (12:1–16:17)	67
❼	Commandments five and six (16:18–22:8)	76
❽	Commandments seven to ten (22:9–26:19)	86
	Part 3 The rite	96
❾	The covenant (27:1–30:20)	97
❿	The successor (31:1–29)	105
⓫	The song (31:30–32:52)	114
⓬	The blessing (33:1–34:12)	122
	Appendix	131
	Endnotes	133
	Further resources	137

8

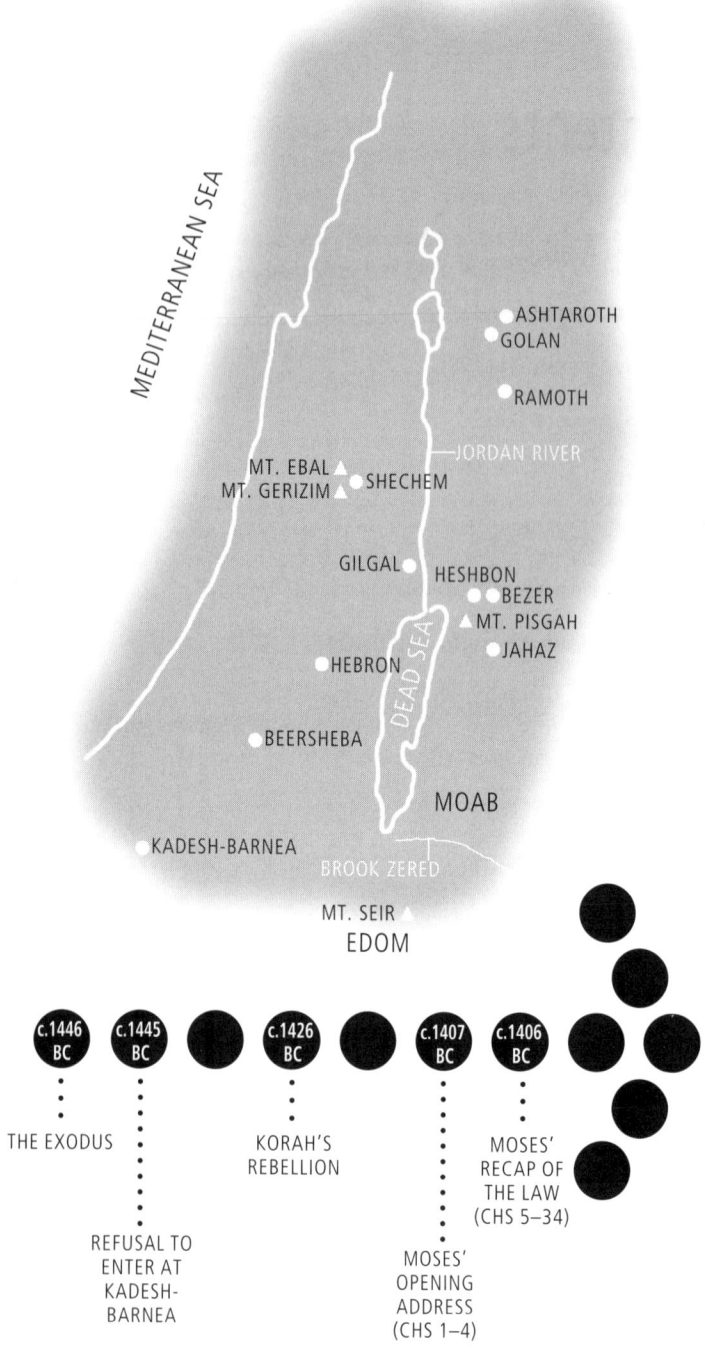

OPENING UP DEUTERONOMY

Background and summary

The Bible is a book of covenants, and Deuteronomy is a covenant book. It isn't 'the book of the covenant'—that title appears to refer to Exodus 20–23 (see Exod. 24:7). Instead, it is a kind of second edition with the words 'Updated & expanded' stamped across the front cover. Or you could think of it as a Covenant 1.02 upgrade ready for life in the promised land.

Covenant author

The Bible leaves us in no doubt that Moses was the author of Deuteronomy. True, there are at least one or two inspired editorial touches[1]—the account of Moses' death being the clearest—but the rest of the Old Testament (Deut. 31:9, 24–26; 1 Kings 2:3; 8:53; 2 Kings 14:6; 18:6, 12), the Lord Jesus (Mark 7:10; 10:3–5; John 7:19) and the apostles Peter and Paul (Acts 3:22; 13:39; 28:23; Rom. 10:5, 19; 1 Cor. 9:9; 2 Cor. 3:15) speak with one voice in crediting Moses as its writer. The book's name, however, doesn't come from Moses. Its Hebrew title was taken from the book's opening (literally, 'These are the words …', Deut. 1:1). 'Deuteronomy'—the name familiar to us and which means 'second law'—was actually based on a mistake. It comes from Jerome's Latin Bible (known as the Vulgate) of about 405 BC, which he translated from the Greek Old Testament (known as the Septuagint). Jerome's translation of 17:18 read 'second law' when the original read 'copy of the law'. Not a great translation, and, let's face it, not an inspiring title either; but it stuck. And it wasn't so bad, in that the whole book is, as I have already mentioned, a kind of second edition. But even the word 'law' isn't ideal. Legal documents aren't usually all that inspiring or relevant. This one is different. It's the kind of contract which calls for a response—and that makes it a covenant.

Covenant themes

The word 'covenant' is used no fewer than twenty-eight times in Deuteronomy and reflects the importance of a theme that dominates the whole book. The covenant that God made with Abraham forms the backdrop for Deuteronomy. In Genesis a land had been promised; in Deuteronomy it is about to be delivered. The first four chapters set the stage for Israel's second attempt to enter the land. Having reminded the people of the unbelief that led to disaster at Kadesh-barnea, Moses encourages them by reminding them of the Lord's faithfulness in giving them initial victories over Sihon and Og east of the Jordan. This time it can and will be a different story.

So some of God's covenant promises to Abraham are in the process of being realized. Next comes a reminder of the covenant declared by Moses at Sinai (4:13), making the point that the Ten Commandments were given with life in the promised land in view (4:14). The covenant mustn't be forgotten (4:23), otherwise they won't last long in Canaan. The covenant with Abraham gave them the land; the covenant from Moses gives the recipe for enjoying the land. And while they need to be warned about the danger of forgetting their covenant obligations, one thing they can be sure of is that the Lord will not forget his covenant promises (4:31). The Ten

Commandments form the heart of the Sinai covenant, and Moses is at pains to point out that it is a covenant still very much in force (5:3). It's a covenant that requires care (5:1, 32), concern (5:29), constancy (5:32) and commitment (5:33); but it also holds out the hope that 'it may go well with' Israel, and that they 'may live long in the land' (5:33). It will all depend on the response of the people. The commandments are given 'that [they] may do them in the land' that they are about to enter (6:1).

The notorious incident of the golden calf casts its shadow over this second covenant declaration. That is why Moses emphasizes the exclusivity of the covenant. No other gods. This Lord stands alone and brooks no rivals (6:4, 15). But this covenant isn't simply a matter of imparting information; it calls for a response. First it needs to be heard (hence the refrain 'Hear, O Israel', 5:1; 6:3–4; 9:1; 20:3), and then it needs to be acted on (5:27; 6:3; 30:12–14). But

> Simple obedience isn't enough: the attitude accompanying obedience is crucial too.

simple obedience isn't enough: the attitude accompanying obedience is crucial too. There should be a reverence and affection for the Lord that ensures his people want to do his will—conveyed in the key words 'fear' (4:10; 5:29; 6:2, 13, 24; 8:6; 10:12, 20; 13:4; 14:23; 17:19; 28:58; 31:12–13), 'serve' (6:13; 10:12, 20; 11:13; 13:4; 28:47, etc.) and 'love' (6:5; 7:9; 10:12; 11:1, 13, 22; 13:3, etc.).

Once in the land there will be many temptations that might lead them away from the straight and narrow. Remaining faithful is the challenge. They will need to stick to God (4:4; 10:20; 11:22; 13:4; 30:20), otherwise they will inevitably turn aside, or, even worse, turn away (5:32; 9:12, 16; 11:16, 28; 17:11, 20; 28:14; 31:29). Before long they will be following after (6:14; 8:19; 11:28; 13:2; 28:14), and ultimately serving, 'other gods' (7:4; 11:16; 13:2, 6, 13; 17:3; 28:14, 36, 64; 29:26; cf. 4:19; 8:19; 30:17), if they aren't *very careful* (2:4; 4:15–16, 19, 23; 5:1, 32; 6:3, 12, 25; 7:11; 8:1, 11, 17; 11:16, 22, 32; 12:1, 13, 19, 28, 30, 32; 15:5, 9; 16:12; 17:10; 19:9; 23:23; 24:8; 26:16; 28:1, 13, 15, 58; 29:18; 31:12; 32:46).

The book reveals to us a 'faithful God who keeps covenant and steadfast love with those who love him' (7:9). The name of God appears in Deuteronomy nearly 200 times. Without a covenant God there would be no covenant. It also tells us what it means to be a covenant people. They are his 'treasured possession' (7:6; 14:2; 26:18) and 'a people holy to the LORD' (7:6; 14:2, 21; 26:19; 28:9)—initially through God's action and initiative, but now to be worked out through their obedience in their everyday lives.

The other big covenant theme is that of the land. We are left in no doubt that it is a 'good land' (1:25, 35; 3:25; 4:21–22; 6:18; 8:7, 10; 9:6; 11:17) that flows 'with milk and honey' (6:3; 11:9; 26:9, 15; 27:3; 31:20). It is also a promised or—more accurately according to the Hebrew—a 'sworn' land (1:8, 35; 4:31; 6:18, 23; 7:8, 12–13; 8:1, 18; 10:11; 11:9, 21; 13:17; 19:8; 26:3, 15; 28:11; 29:12; 30:20; 31:7, 20–21, 23). The land can be seen from two very different angles captured by two recurring phrases. It is a land 'which the LORD your God gives to you' (used thirty-four times), but it is also a 'land you are to possess' (twenty-two times). It is a divine gift, but it is Israel's responsibility to conquer. And obedience will then be the key to Israel's continuing enjoyment of the land.

Covenant commandments

The giving of the law in Moab isn't just a reminder and reinforcement of the earlier covenant. Moses goes on to explain and expand on those commandments with particular reference to the new life awaiting them across the Jordan. As he does so the principle that lies behind each commandment is brought out and then applied to specific circumstances they will soon be facing. The first commandment is a call to devotion—to wholeheartedly love and obey the one and only true God. The second commandment is a call to worship by the book—in the right place, in the right way and with the right resolve. The third commandment spells out the responsibility that comes with bearing the Lord's name: to be holy. There needs to be a double commitment—to steer clear of anything that could in anyway defile them, and to be consistently God-fearing in a way that has practical and even financial implications. Commandment number four contains a principle that is to be applied to the new society that will be established in the land: they must remember the Sabbath year, as well as the Sabbath day. This will have a huge impact on poverty, slavery and husbandry. The three great annual feasts of Passover, Weeks and Booths are other seasons to be observed, giving Israel strategic reminders in the course of each year of God's goodness to them.

Commandment five is also expanded. Moses extends it beyond parents, applying the authority principle to judges, prophets, priests and kings as well. The sixth commandment outlaws murder, but Moses shows that the basic principle that life is sacred needs to be applied to issues surrounding manslaughter, war, disputes, the death penalty and safety. With the seventh commandment the core principle is that of purity, both sexual and ceremonial. Commandment eight concerns property, encouraging us to respect the belongings of others while not holding on to our own possessions too tightly. Fairness and justice for all, particularly in the context of civil disputes, is the focus in applying the ninth commandment. Last, but not least, the final commandment prohibiting covetousness is shown to be a matter of the heart —closely linked with thankfulness and contentment.

Covenant structure

Not only does the book of Deuteronomy have a covenant theme and covenant commandments, it also has a covenant structure. It is set out as a formal document—what we would think of as a contract—following the pattern of contemporary treaties between nations.[2] Much as Paul took a standard letter of his day and adapted it slightly for his purposes while retaining the traditional constituent parts, Moses has drawn up an agreement between the Lord and his people according to the custom of the time. It looks like this:

PREAMBLE (1:1–5)
A simple introduction recording the time and place of the agreement.
PROLOGUE (1:6–4:43)
A section that puts the agreement in its historical context.
PRECEPTS (4:44–26:19)

The conditions of the agreement are stated, with the specific requirements set out clearly. This is followed by a more detailed explanation of each requirement in turn.[3]

PROVISOS (27:1–28:68)

The penalties for breaking the agreement are stated, along with the promises attached if the conditions are met.

PROPOSAL (29:1–30:20)

Here the covenant is proposed to the people as something to choose and commit themselves to.

PROVISION (31:1–33:29)

Provision is made in this section for the future observance of the agreement. The main elements are regular readings of the law and the appointment of a successor to Moses. An element of prophecy is also included, clearly predicting the faithfulness of the Lord and the faithlessness of his people. Promises are also provided—in the form of blessings—for each of the tribes, regarding the challenges of the future.

PROSPECT (34:1–12)

In the final chapter Moses is given a prospect of the promised land, even though he won't be allowed in. And the prospect for Israel looks good, as Moses' authority and spiritual wisdom are transferred to Joshua.

Covenant commitment

The danger of talking about formal documents and structures is that we might get the impression that Deuteronomy presents us with something of purely academic interest. Nothing could be further from the truth. It is a book calling for commitment. God has brought his people to the land of Moab where a decision needs to be made. The book ensures that Israel are not left in the dark as to what that decision entails. And it is a decision that can't be put off. It needs to be made '*today*' (a word used over fifty times[4]).

Covenant influence

The influence of the book of Deuteronomy on the rest of Scripture is hard to overstate and easy to underestimate. Quotations from and allusions to Deuteronomy are everywhere in the rest of the Old Testament. It could be argued that the role of most of the subsequent prophets was to call Israel back to the law delivered by Moses, and to covenant obedience. Isaiah and Jeremiah especially were clearly steeped in the words and teachings of Deuteronomy.

> The influence of the book of Deuteronomy on the rest of Scripture is hard to overstate and easy to underestimate.

When we get to the New Testament we find that the strong influence continues. There are many quotations and allusions found in over two-thirds of the books of the New Testament (see Appendix). Paul, as you would expect of a Pharisee (Phil. 3:5), clearly has Deuteronomy in his blood, but most striking of all is the use of the book by the Lord Jesus. Judging from the number of times he quotes from it, you could argue that Deuteronomy was his favourite book (Matt. 4:4, 7, 10; 5:21, 27, 31, 38; 15:4; 18:16; 19:18–19; 22:37; Mark 7:10; 10:19; 12:29–30, 33; Luke 4:4, 8, 12; 18:20).

Then there is the influence the book has on the New Testament's teaching regarding a 'new covenant' (Luke 22:20;

1 Cor. 11:25; 2 Cor. 3:6; Heb. 8:8, 13; 9:15; 12:24). There are important differences, of course (Heb. 8:9–13), but there are also many similarities. In the gospel the Lord has similarly taken the initiative in a work of redemption. This new covenant calls for the same pattern of obedient response to the commandments of its mediator (Heb. 9:15; Matt. 28:20; John 14:15, 21, 23). The motivation should also be the same: love and gratitude. Israel had seen how the Lord had brought them 'out of the land of Egypt, out of the house of slavery' (Deut. 5:6). We have seen the cross.

For further study ▶

FOR FURTHER STUDY

1. Find out where the titles 'Old and New Testament' come from. Why not call them the Old and New Covenant?
2. Read Matthew 4:1–11. What do you think is the basic issue with each of the temptations? In what ways is our Saviour's use of Deuteronomy surprising, and how does it shed light on the context of the verses quoted and the temptations themselves?
3. How many different covenants does the Bible tell us about? Are they connected in any way?

TO THINK ABOUT AND DISCUSS

1. Often the promised land is seen as a picture of heaven. What are the problems with this approach? Is there a better approach, with practical implications for our lives today?
2. What are the main similarities between the old and new covenants, and what are the most important differences?
3. Can you think of important contemporary applications of the last six commandments that could easily be missed if we just took them literally rather than as key principles?

Part 1
The review

1 The rebellion

(1:1–46)

Geographically, the people of Israel are on the threshold of the promised land, and historically, they are on the verge of a new chapter in the nation's life. It's time to take stock. Lessons from the past need to be learned, warnings about the future need to be heeded, and there are promises they will need to trust if they are to go forward. And this time[1] they must go forward—along the path of obedience.

Challenges lie ahead, and Moses realizes that Israel will need a healthy dose of two ingredients as they go forward: humility and faith. There is a gentle reminder in these opening verses of how they came to be where they are at this particular point in time. An eleven-day journey has taken them forty years to complete (vv. 2–3)! Like the chief butler in Joseph's time, Israel has good cause to say, 'I remember my offences today!' (Gen. 41:9). Past mistakes—no, let's call them what they were: past *sins*—should have meant present humility. The same goes for us. The only thing sin is good for is helping to humble us—and when it comes to humility, we need all the help we can get.

Time to leave (1:1–18)

Moses is addressing the people 'In the fortieth year' (v. 3). Even those forty years—the result of Israel's unbelief—were not without further sin and failure. But this was a period when the Lord had demonstrated wonderful examples of his faithfulness to his people. Victories over Sihon, king of the Amorites, and Og, king of Bashan (v. 4), would be remembered in prayer and celebrated in praise down through the centuries (Neh. 9:22; Ps. 136:17–22). They were a kind of 'firstfruits'—symbolic victories to be seen as the first of many; tokens of what was to come.

Moses now reminds them of their marching orders when the call came from the Lord telling them it was time to leave Horeb (vv. 6–8).[2] Yes, they had a journey ahead of them, but it was their destination that really mattered. They had been brought out of Egypt that they might 'go in' (v. 8) to the promised land. Moses had set it before them (v. 8, as well as the Lord, v. 21) by way of promise, and now it is set before them geographically, and perhaps visually too, given the view from Mount Nebo. Of course, this wasn't a land that they could just wander into unopposed. They would need to 'take possession' of it.

It had been at that point that the wisdom of delegating some of Moses' responsibilities had, through the advice of his father-in-law, become apparent. It was a good problem to have. The extent of the burden upon Moses was, in itself, evidence of the Lord's blessing. The number of Abraham's descendants had been promised long before, so here was evidence of the Lord's faithfulness (v. 10). And the promise still had mileage left in it, as Moses made clear: there would be more growth to come (v. 11). Only in the time of Solomon would Israel reach numbers that were like the sand on the seashore or the stars in the Middle-Eastern night sky. Only then would it be said that they were too numerous to count (1 Kings 3:8).

However, although a reason for thanksgiving, it was still a problem. Burnout isn't a new problem. It can be the fault of people demanding too much of one man, or it can be a failure to delegate on the part of the individual, but the end result is the same. Of course, rusting out—failing to do what we can—is no better. Lasting out—what Paul called 'finishing the race' (2 Tim. 4:7)—should be the aim. Knowing our limitations will help, and, failing that, learning to spot the warning signs which indicate we are overdoing it can also alert us to the need to slow down.

Sheer weight of work is one thing, but 'strife' (v. 12) is quite another. If large numbers were a good problem to have, the same can't be said of conflict. It can make the meekest man in the world lose his temper (Num. 12:3). Few things wear a leader down more than internal squabbles. When Paul spoke about his 'anxiety for all the churches' (2 Cor. 11:28) we know that 'divisions' and 'quarrelling' were among his concerns (1 Cor. 1:10–11; see also Rom. 16:17; Phil. 4:2; Titus 3:10).

One characteristic above all others is needed in a good judge: impartiality (vv. 16–17). Showing favouritism to one group or class over another is often where strife begins and injustice follows. Riches, fame, and the like can easily either intimidate or intoxicate. Judges need to be God-fearing in order to make sure that they are unimpressed by anyone else. Whether the prejudice is to do with age, education, wealth, appearance or popularity, it often boils down to whether people are like or unlike us. Iustitia (the Roman goddess of justice) is nearly always depicted blindfold in works of art to make the same point Moses makes here. At the time of writing, a reality TV programme being shown works on the same principle. The judging criterion is the quality of the entrant's singing voice. The judges don't actually get to see the entrant when he or she auditions, ensuring that they concentrate on the voice alone, unswayed by appearances.

> Judges need to be God-fearing in order to make sure that they are unimpressed by anyone else.

The emphasis on the judges' delegated authority was also a timely reminder to Israel that their judges should be respected. The authority they had been given was not a temporary arrangement for the journey, but was to be equally respected once they had taken possession of the land.

Time to enter (1:19–33)

Next comes a reminder that must have been a lot more painful. They had requested a spying expedition, which seemed, even to Moses, to be a good idea at the time. It would later become apparent that the suggestion had sprung from the beginnings of unbelief. Postponing obedience is all too often a 'playing for time' tactic, designed to make ultimate disobedience seem less outrageous. While we have an unhappy natural ability to recognize all the extenuating circumstances that surround our falls into sin, true confession has a different outlook. To properly repent of our sins we need first to see them in all their ugliness, warts and all, with all the aggravations that make them that much worse. The spies' admission that the land was good (v. 25) should have reinforced their faith in the God who had promised them that it would be. But they didn't want to believe, because they didn't want to 'go up' (v. 26). Moses makes clear that this wasn't just a case of faint-heartedness; this was rebellion 'against the command of the Lord'; and it didn't stop there, because they also 'murmured' against the Lord himself (v. 27). They questioned his goodness and love. This is what the devil has been doing ever since the garden of Eden (Gen. 3:5), and it is never a good sign when we follow suit. Moses seeks to remind them how the goodness and love of God has been demonstrated to them (vv. 29–31). The Lord fought for them against Pharaoh, and then, having brought them out of Egypt, he carried them across the wilderness. Couldn't they trust a God like that, even when fortified cities and giant enemies stood in their way?

Time to wander (1:34–46)

They had murmured in their tents, but the Lord heard (v. 34). They could have murmured in their hearts and it would have made no difference. Sometimes our words anger the Lord. A God who gets angry isn't everybody's cup of tea. Many people say that 'My God doesn't get angry', but the only honest response is to point out (graciously!) that their God can't be the

God of the Bible. If he is the one true God (and he is!), their idea of God is an idol, tailor-made to their own specifications, but an idol all the same. What's more, we have a Saviour who gets angry too. We need to be careful to distinguish divine anger from the human kind we are all too familiar with. Our anger tends to be an outburst of annoyance at the fact that, in one way or another, our will has been thwarted. It's often arbitrary and inconsistent, usually selfish, and rarely characterized by self-control. As Aristotle once said, '… any one can get angry—that is easy … but to do this to the right person, to the right extent, at the right time, with the right motive, and in the right way, that is not for every one, nor is it easy.'[3] The Bible challenge is put simply by the psalmist and the apostle Paul: 'Be angry and do not sin' (Eph. 4:26; Ps. 37:8). Our Saviour's anger with the money-changers in the temple (John 2:14–16) or with the Pharisees' hardness of heart (Mark 3:5) was a display of *divine* anger. It was principled and controlled, with wickedness as its object. It wasn't personal irritation, but a settled attitude of hostility towards sin rightly identified and assessed. Many today think of God as indulgent towards sin, but the Bible tells us that he is actually indignant against sin. His anger is absolutely right, and helps us get the measure of sin's seriousness. For us, though, the old saying is true: 'Anger is only one letter short of danger.'

Though God is slow to anger, once his anger is kindled discipline of some sort will not be far behind. Often that discipline is especially tailored to fit the crime and to underline the lesson that needs to be learned. When our words or thoughts spring from sin and unbelief, they may well come back to haunt us. That was the case for Moses himself when he spoke 'rashly' (Ps. 106:33), although in Deuteronomy 1 Moses reminds Israel of their provoking role in his sin. With Israel, what they in their unbelief feared for their children would be their own experience instead.

On a brighter note, when our words are fuelled by faith, the Lord hears them just as clearly. Caleb's confidence in God shone all the brighter against the backdrop of Israel's unbelief (v. 36). While the Lord's people often provoke him, it is possible to please him, and Caleb shows us how. He 'wholly followed the LORD': what a great epitaph to have! And he had it in triplicate (Deut. 1:36; Num. 14:24; 32:12). He followed the Lord fully (literally, 'to the full') despite the pressure of ten fellow spies and the sight of Canaan's walls and giants. As someone has said, 'Ten men saw the city walls and their faith crumbled; two men had faith and lived to see the walls crumble.' It had been a simple (though not easy) matter of obedience. Faith is often a matter of trusting as we obey, despite the possible consequences we can foresee.

> **Faith is often a matter of trusting as we obey, despite the possible consequences we can foresee.**

A pilot was once having trouble landing his plane and needed the help of the control tower. As they radioed their instructions, the inexperienced pilot objected, 'But there's a pole there.' This lack of trust met with the reply, 'You take care of the instructions and we'll take care of the obstructions.' The Lord was effectively saying the same to Israel, but only Caleb and Joshua would listen. Even Moses had failed to follow instructions when he struck the rock instead of speaking to it

(Num. 20:8, 10–11), and it cost him dear. A whole generation, bar two, would miss out, but the children they wouldn't trust to God's protection would prove his faithfulness (v. 39).

Israel's reply to Moses' reproof was no better than their initial response. They should have 'taken their medicine' and humbly accepted the Lord's discipline. Instead they tried to avoid it, but the rebellious spirit was the same, this time in the form of presumption (v. 43). First they doubted the promise, then they dismissed the warning.

It was always going to end in tears, and in this instance the tears were literal (v. 45). Literal, but not acceptable. These were not tears of repentance but of self-pity. It is possible to think that if we cry about something, all must be well and the Lord's sympathy is assured; but it all depends on what we are crying about and why. Good tears are a blessing, and we are assured that God registers each drop and stores it in a bottle for safe-keeping (Ps. 56:8). Nevertheless, there is a 'worldly grief', as Paul makes clear to the Corinthians (2 Cor. 7:10).

Good tears adorn our prayers, but the wrong kind can render our prayers null and void, as happens here. When we go wrong—badly, wilfully, repeatedly wrong—it may be 'many days' (v. 46) before we get back on track. That's where Moses wants the people to be, and where we need to be too: back on track.

For further study ▶

FOR FURTHER STUDY

1. What biblical examples can you think of where particular sins have had a lasting humbling effect on somebody (or even on a nation)?
2. Find as many examples as you can of strife in the churches of the New Testament epistles. What were they about, and what would you identify as the main cause?
3. Read Proverbs 10:12; 13:10; 15:18; 16:28; 17:1, 14, 19; 26:21; 29:22. What lessons can we learn about strife from these proverbs?
4. Read Ezra 9:6–15; Nehemiah 9:32–37; and Daniel 9:5–19. How many aggravating factors regarding Israel's sins are mentioned, and what are they?
5. Read Exodus 15:22–25; 16:2–3; 17:1–3; Numbers 14:1–4; 16:39–41. What gave rise to grumbling in Israel?
6. Read John 2:13–17; Mark 3:1–6; and Matthew 21:18–19. What was Jesus particularly angry about in these instances, and what might be modern-day equivalents?
7. Read 2 Corinthians 7:8–11. What are the key differences between godly and worldly grief?

TO THINK ABOUT AND DISCUSS

1. What causes of strife can you identify that often affect churches today? How many of them are doctrinal, and how many practical?
2. What do you find yourself 'murmuring' about most often? What are the main areas of your life which cause you to murmur, and why do you think that is?
3. Are you postponing obedience in any area of your life at the moment?
4. What do you tend to get angry about in a wrong way, and what do you think it is right to get angry about?
5. When was the last time you confessed to God, and asked forgiveness for, something that you *thought*?

2 The wilderness

(2:1–3:29)

Israel's rebellion meant that they had to face punishment, but not abandonment. There were rules for the journey, but as they followed the Lord's lead they were kept and sustained. As their wanderings drew to a close the Lord gave them two faith-strengthening victories just before the baton was passed from Moses to Joshua.

Sovereign over international boundaries (2:1–25)

Their punishment was painful and prolonged, but it didn't last for ever. The word from the Lord to leave the area around Mount Seir meant that the end of their wanderings was in sight. Even so, there was still difficult and dangerous territory to be negotiated (particularly the lands of Edom and Moab—see map in the 'Background and Summary' chapter). Not that their safety posed any problem for the Lord of all the earth. Esau (Edom), Moab and Ammon were just three of 'the peoples who [were] under the whole heaven' (v. 25). The Lord would ensure that the people of Esau were afraid of Israel (v. 4). This would no doubt have rung bells with Moses and the people. Dealing with danger from Esau was something the Lord had done before. Way back in Genesis, Jacob had fled from his brother Esau in fear of his life, having tricked him out of his father's blessing (Gen. 27:42). Years later, having been on the receiving end of trickery at Laban's hands, he headed back to the land of his family. But what about Esau? The last thing Jacob knew, his brother was planning to kill him; but then he got news that Esau was on his way to meet him. It was a situation that drove Jacob to his knees, confessing his fear and asking for deliverance (Gen. 32:9–12). A happy reunion followed—Jacob's prayer had been wonderfully answered!

Israel had to resist the temptation to fear the people of Esau, but they needed also to resist the temptation to take advantage of their old enemies' alarm and attack them. They weren't even to exploit the situation for material gain, but must give a fair price for food and drink (vv. 4–6). The people of God don't need to be money-grabbing when they have such a generous God with them to supply their needs. He can do it miraculously with manna or unspectacularly via the supermarket, but the source is the same. When the Lord is our Shepherd we can be confident that we will 'not want' (Ps. 23:1).

I was once amused to read about an American pastor who let his local newspaper know the titles of his sermons a week in advance so that they could be advertised. One week he was planning to preach on Psalm 23 and gave the rather unimaginative title 'The Lord's My Shepherd'. When the editor asked him whether there was anything else, he innocently replied, 'No, "The Lord's My Shepherd"; that's enough.' To his surprise and delight, what appeared in the paper that week was, 'The Lord's My Shepherd: That's Enough!' The editor had unwittingly improved the title.

There was a promised land for Israel, but it wasn't Mount Seir. Neither was it Ar (v. 9) or Ammon (v. 19). They were to be content with the land allotted to them.

Contentment is 'a rare jewel', as the Puritan Jeremiah Burroughs once put it, and it doesn't come naturally. The grass does have a way of looking greener on the other side of the fence and it can save us a lot of trouble if we keep that in mind. Truly appreciating what the Lord has given or promised to us is an important step in the right direction. It was when Israel forgot about the promised milk and honey that they began to remember the leeks and onions of Egypt (Num. 11:5). The strange thing is that having plenty is no safeguard against being discontented; if anything, it makes it more likely. It is a bit like the millionaire who, when asked how much it took to be happy, smiled and answered, 'Just a little bit more.' King Ahab no doubt had much land, but he wanted Naboth's vineyard (1 Kings 21:1–4). King David (to his shame) had many wives and concubines, but he wanted

> **The strange thing is that having plenty is no safeguard against being discontented.**

Bathsheba (2 Sam. 11:2–4). They both serve as warnings of where discontentment can lead. What Israel needed was the attitude of David in better times: 'The lines have fallen for me in pleasant places' (Ps. 16:6).

Israel also needed to be patient until the Lord, in his time, brought them into the land. It is so easy, when faced with frustrating delays, to take matters into our own hands. And trying to hurry things along can often involve us adopting questionable methods—like someone in a traffic jam deciding to use the hard shoulder; or Abraham opting for a child with Hagar, rather than waiting and trusting God (Gen. 16:1–4). King Saul gave in to impatience as he waited for Samuel, and made offerings to the Lord which would prove to be the beginning of the end for his reign (1 Sam. 10:8; 13:8–14). His successor, David, in contrast, showed commendable patience as he waited for God's time for him to take the throne, refusing to dispose of Saul even when presented with two golden opportunities (1 Sam. 24:6–7; 26:9–11).

> **Trying to hurry things along can often involve us adopting questionable methods.**

Israel needed to count their blessings and wait upon the Lord, and so do we. These are two big themes in the songs of Israel, so the book of Psalms can help us in both areas. There was also the danger of settling for second best, rather than pressing on for all that the Lord had in store for them according to his promise. We should be content with what we've got, but never content with where we're at in the Christian life.

Just because the Lord had blessed them in a special way, it didn't mean that they could do what they liked. It meant that they should do what *he* liked. They needed to follow the path of obedience, confident that it would also prove to be the path of greatest blessing. Later in Deuteronomy we will be reminded that 'he fixed the borders of the peoples' (32:8) and that those borders needed to be respected. Paul also speaks of how God 'made from one man every nation of mankind to live on all the face of the earth, having determined allotted periods and the boundaries of their dwelling place' (Acts 17:26). Admittedly, it's easy to lose sight of God's sovereignty when we see how the greed and violence of people are the more obvious factors in deciding who lives where. Nonetheless, his purposes are being worked out in and through the conflicts of sinful people. To him, Isaiah reminds us, 'the nations are like a drop from a bucket, and are accounted as the dust on the scales' (Isa. 40:15).

As Israel passed through Edom, Moab and Ammon one lesson should have been impressed on their minds and hearts three times over. The Lord had dispossessed the Horites, the Emim and the Rephaim in the past (vv. 11–12). Surely he could dispossess the Canaanites in the same way! What's more, the Emim and the Rephaim were 'a people great and many, and tall as the Anakim' (vv. 10, 21) but that had not proved a problem to the Lord. They should have listened to Caleb thirty-eight years before: 'he will bring us into this land and give it to us' (Num. 14:8). Maybe they would believe their eyes as they negotiated enemy territory that had previously belonged to giants.

Sovereign over international conflicts (2:26–3:11)

The Lord's gracious faith-strengthening exercise for what lay ahead now went up a notch. Having safely traversed hostile terrain they were now to get their first taste of conflict. The entire generation of men of war whose nerve had failed at Kadesh-barnea had perished (2:16). The Lord had been faithful to his warning. Now there was a new generation, and the Lord gave them a gentle introduction to the harsh realities of war. He set their enemies trembling (2:24–25). The Lord had been faithful to the promise of Moses' prophecy, too (Exod. 15:14–16). Victory followed (2:33–36), and then came a bigger test for Israel. The Lord gave them further reassurance ahead of the more daunting clash with Og: 'you shall do to him as you did to Sihon' (3:2). Never mind the fact that he was a giant and that his cities were fortified with 'high walls, gates and bars' (3:5).

Sovereign over men's hearts (2:26–3:29)

There is more encouragement for the people of Israel in Moses' account of the exchange with Sihon before the battle. Moses didn't pick a fight with Sihon; he respectfully requested free passage, with the very reasonable promise of payment for provisions (2:26–29). Why didn't Sihon see sense and accept the generous terms? The explanation is simple and significant: the Lord 'hardened his spirit and made his heart obstinate' (2:30). Just as their long journey had begun—with the hardening of Pharaoh's heart—so it was coming to an end, with the Lord demonstrating his sovereignty over the heart of another individual. We read a number of times that Pharaoh hardened his own heart, and then at other times that the Lord hardened it. We see what is happening from two different perspectives. On the one hand, Pharaoh was responsible for his sinful attitude of heart. On the other, the Lord was judicially giving him up to the hardness he had chosen. The 'iniquity of the Amorites' was now full (see Gen. 15:16) and so God's judgement was about to fall. The Lord righteously ensured that Sihon's response to Moses' request was the one that came naturally to him—an obstinate one. So the hard heart was an initial part of the judgement.

God is at work in the hearts of individuals to ensure that his gracious purposes for his people reach fruition. 'The king's heart [whether it be Pharaoh's, Sihon's, Nebuchadnezzar's, Cyrus's or Herod's] is a stream of water in the hand of the Lord; he turns it wherever he will' (Prov. 21:1).

With the firstfruits of military victory came the firstfruits of the land, albeit east of the Jordan. Before settling there, though, the two and a half tribes who were given this land needed to fight alongside their brothers until the other tribes were safely installed in their lands to the west (3:18–20).

It must have been a bittersweet moment for Moses. The taste of victory must have been tempered by the disappointment that he was not to enter the land himself. His prayer was answered just as many of ours are: half of his prayer was granted, the other denied. To the request 'Please let me go over' (3:25) came the emphatic response 'you shall not go over' (3:27). We sometimes talk about 'unanswered prayer' when it would be more accurate to speak of 'denied prayer'. The answer 'No' is really an answer! Long before Jesus prayed in Gethsemane or Paul prayed about his thorn in the flesh, Moses had to learn this for himself. If we are following the Saviour's example and qualifying our requests with a genuinely heartfelt 'Nevertheless, not my will, but yours, be done' (Luke 22:42), we should take a 'No' in our stride. If we are treating prayer as a way of ensuring that we get our own way, a 'No' will be a lot harder to take. However, even when our prayers are somewhat misguided, God delights to 'give good things to those who ask him' (Matt. 7:11), and so to Moses' request 'Please let me go over and see …' came the answer 'Go up … and look' (3:27). Thankfully, Moses was the meekest of men (Num. 12:3), and so, despite his disappointment, he accepted the Lord's will and set about preparing his successor. Much as David graciously submitted to God when told that he was not to build the temple, and set about giving every help to Solomon, so Moses was careful to 'encourage and strengthen' Joshua (3:28). He began by making sure that Joshua drew out all the confidence-building encouragement he could from the double victory God had given (3:21–22). He knew that fear is the enemy, and that faith—faith in 'the LORD your God who fights for you' (3:22)—is the antidote. There would be many battles to come for Joshua, and he would need to remember these examples of God's sufficiency. Moses, though, had all but 'fought the good fight … finished the race [and] kept the faith' (2 Tim. 4:7).

FOR FURTHER STUDY

1. Read Genesis 32:9–21. What can we learn from this prayer about dealing with fear? What action did Jacob take as well as praying? Do you think that was wise or a sign of unbelief, and why?
2. Read Hebrews 13:5–6. What should help us be content according to these two verses?
3. Read Psalm 103. How many blessings can you count, and what kinds of blessings were most important to David?
4. Read Psalm 25:1–5, 16–21; 37:1–10, 34. When the psalmist talks about 'waiting' on the Lord, what do you think he is waiting for, and how does he say we should wait?
5. Read 2 Samuel 15:31; 17:1–14. How does the Lord answer David's prayer?

TO THINK ABOUT AND DISCUSS

1. Have you ever suffered from 'the grass is greener' syndrome, and have you learnt from it?
2. Which areas of your life are most affected by discontentment? What do you think you can do about it?
3. Have you ever noticed yourself hardening your heart against anyone? How might we spot the hardening of our hearts towards God?
4. What might help us keep our hearts soft? What are the signs that a heart is soft?

3 The warning

(4:1–43)

We've almost got to the second reading of the law, but first Moses is keen to highlight the great blessings that will follow from keeping the commandments. At the same time he underlines the number one danger that they will face in the promised land: idolatry!

Before Moses again sets out the law, he stresses that what he will be committing to them comes as a whole. It will be no pick-and-mix, where you can choose to follow the laws that suit you and ignore the rest. Budding Pharisees will want to add their own extra rules, while the majority will feel more comfortable just doing a bit of editing. But these are 'the commandments of the LORD [our] God' (v. 2) and as such need no alteration. Adding to a perfect law or subtracting from it are equally wrong and equally serious (Rev. 22:18–19). It's always good to keep an eye on the unwritten rules of 'acceptability' in different churches and traditions. We might be surprised how many of them have little to do with biblical laws and principles. It can also beggar belief how skilfully some Christians and denominations manage to explain away or simply ignore clear biblical commands. The Saviour's warning to 'whoever relaxes one of the least of these commandments' (Matt. 5:19) ought to give us pause for thought. To be careful to obey the minutiae of God's law was not what the Pharisees got wrong; Jesus said, 'These you ought to have done' (Matt. 23:23). It was neglecting 'the weightier matters of the law' that was the problem. Partial obedience actually amounts to disobedience, whichever precepts we fall foul of. Someone has cautioned against the 'dip and skip' method of Christian living—dipping into God's promises while skipping his commands. The commandments are to be preserved in their entirety, so that they may be observed in their entirety.

What they saw at Baal-peor (4:1–10)

Moses wants the people to 'live' (v. 1), and the way to do that is to listen to the law. He will put the choice to the people even more starkly towards the end of the book (see 30:11–20), but for now his example of what happened at Baal-peor makes it clear that this is a matter of life and death. Follow a false god and you will follow him to destruction; hold fast to the Lord and he will hold you fast (vv. 3–4). If you answer his call to obedience, he will be 'on call' to respond to your cries 24/7 (v. 7).

Baal-peor was Israel's most recent failure at this point and would still have been fresh in the memory of many of those Moses was addressing. There they had experienced the 'fierce anger' (Num. 25:4) of the Lord, and the solemn scenes of execution that followed must have stayed with those who had witnessed them or even participated in them. The plague must also have left its mark (Num. 25:8–9), as did Phinehas' zeal. It was an episode that Israel was not meant to forget—ever. It became part of their history and hymnology (Ps. 106:28), a prime example of their unfaithfulness (Hosea 9:10), but also a standing warning of idolatry's consequences.

When God's people are obedient their example acts as a witness to those around them. The world is watching them, Moses tells Israel, and their testimony will be effective just as long as they keep and do the commandments (vv. 6–8). And if the Lord told Israel, 'You are my witnesses', the Lord Jesus tells his followers that they are too (Acts 1:8). What Israel was to be to the surrounding nations, Christians are to be wherever they are. We are called to be salt and light, with the aim of bringing glory to God (Matt. 5:13–16; 1 Peter 2:9, 12).

But it's not just for the nations' benefit that Israel need to set a good example. The succeeding generations also feature prominently throughout Deuteronomy. The commandments need to be lived, but they also need to be taught—and not only to our children, but also to our children's children (v. 9). I don't know who was first to point it out, but the church is always only one generation from extinction. It is very easy to demote teaching in the church's priorities, but we do so at our peril, as the New Testament stresses time and again. We could and should have learned its importance from the Old Testament, even as far back as the call of Abraham in Genesis (Gen. 18:19).

Fallen men and women have a problem with amnesia. Our past experiences should be remembered, and the lessons learned need to be stored in our hearts. Instead, we tend to forget, and to retain very little. Forgetting God is a kind of practical atheism which can lead to behaviour of the very worst kind. In a lecture in 1983 the Russian dissident Alexander Solzhenitsyn said this:

> Over half a century ago, while I was still a child, I recall hearing a number of old people offer the following explanation for the great disasters that had befallen Russia: 'Men have forgotten God; that's why all this has happened.' Since then I have spent well-nigh fifty years working on the history of our revolution; in the process I have read hundreds of books, collected hundreds of personal testimonies, and have already contributed eight volumes of my own toward the effort of clearing away the rubble left by that upheaval. But if I were asked today to formulate as concisely as possible the main cause of the ruinous revolution that swallowed up some sixty million of our people, I could not put it more accurately than to repeat: 'Men have forgotten God; that's why all this has happened.'[1]

Forgetting is a theme that Moses will return to again and again in Deuteronomy to help us not forget about the dangers of forgetting! Our memory for important spiritual lessons is so bad that even having witnessed striking events laden with significance is no guarantee that we will remember.

What they didn't see at Horeb[2] (4:10–43)

Having reminded them of what they saw at Baal-peor, Moses goes on to stress what they *didn't* see at Sinai: they didn't see the Lord. They *heard* him, but they didn't *see* him. They saw 'no form' (v. 12). The religions around them focused on 'forms', or 'idols', so there was a huge temptation to copy them. Only a few decades before there had been the infamous incident of the golden calf. This was a danger that needed to be stressed, even before it was placed at the head of the Ten Commandments. The Lord had delivered them from Egypt and, in doing so, had delivered them from idolatry. Many (and perhaps all) of the plagues were related to the idolatrous practices of Pharaoh and his countrymen. Israel are supposed to have left all that behind—for good. Life in the promised land was to be different. The people had a privilege that Moses had been denied; but with the privilege came a weighty responsibility. That's how covenants worked; penalties were attached in case the requirements were not kept. The God they had entered into covenant with was a jealous God (v. 24), and that had major implications. He wouldn't just be an idle spectator if they broke their side of the agreement; their God would get angry, not in a bad-tempered way, but it would mean destruction and exile. To make matters worse (and they would only have themselves to blame), they would find themselves in the midst of wood and stone idols ill-equipped to help them (v. 28). Having been delivered from the iron furnace of Egypt, they would end up experiencing their God as a consuming fire. They would have been brought out of the frying pan only to cast themselves into the fire of God's anger. The promise that they would enter the land was unconditional, but how long they would get to enjoy it very much depended on their obedience.

There is undoubtedly a prophetic element to the warning in verses 25–31. We can't be sure whether Moses actually knew that this was what the future held, but the Spirit under whose inspiration he spoke certainly did. God's jealousy meant that this was no idle threat; but God's mercy was just as real, making the covenant promise that there would be a future reconciliation equally reliable (vv. 29–31). Of course, jealousy and mercy are qualities that both have their source in love (see v. 37). True love will produce anger when the loved one is unfaithful, but it will also show mercy when the same person seeks forgiveness. Forget the covenant, and Israel would find God to be a consuming fire. Return to him in obedience and they would find a merciful, faithful God ready to receive them.

So what's the big deal about idolatry? In short, no form or image can do justice to the God of Israel. He is unique and quite literally incomparable (vv. 32–35). You can't compare him to anything else without in some way diminishing him. The Bible helps us to understand certain aspects of his character through comparisons, but these comparisons are never to be taken on their own as adequate expressions of who he is or what he is like. Israel's God was nothing like the gods of the nations around them.

But it wasn't just about images. There is a subtler form of idolatry that is less obvious but no less damaging to our relationship with God. Anything that takes first place in our lives at God's expense has become an idol. As John Calvin pointed out centuries ago, the heart of every man or woman is 'an idol factory'. Twenty-first-century idols try to fly under the radar but are every bit as demanding as Baal

OPENING UP DEUTERONOMY

or Molech. Hedonism (pleasure-worship) and materialism (stuff-worship) are perhaps the most popular, though we can also worship security, power, popularity, respectability, excitement, and a host of other things. Many of them boil down to narcissism—the worship of self. Whatever the idols are, the idolater is the loser. As Jonah pointed out, 'Those who pay regard to vain idols forsake their hope of steadfast love' (Jonah 2:8). Mind you, it took his being swallowed by a big fish to bring him to his senses!

Not only is Israel's God unique; Moses stresses that Israel's relationship with God is unique as well. It began with a unique series of events. Just as in creation, the redemption of Israel began with God speaking (v. 33). He was no dumb idol. And then their redemption was accomplished through the action of God. When this God acted it was with 'a mighty hand and an outstretched arm' (v. 34). No other gods were in the same league as 'the LORD'. Just the fact that the people were still alive, having heard and seen him, was evidence of his love. Then there were the plagues, the pillars of cloud and fire, and the dividing of the Red Sea too. What more did they need? Surely this Lord was indisputably 'God in heaven above and on the earth beneath' (v. 39). That's why he should be obeyed. Really, that ought to be enough, but there was the added incentive that blessing and the duration of their time in the land also hung on their obedience.

This section ends with Moses designating three places east of the Jordan as cities of refuge (vv. 41–43). This was a merciful provision that upheld the sanctity of life while recognizing that accidents do happen. They are distributed carefully among the two and a half tribes to ensure that they are accessible to all. The east of the Jordan is sorted out; now the west awaits …

For further study ▶

FOR FURTHER STUDY

1. Read Matthew 23:1–28. What sorts of laws did the Pharisees add to God's laws, and why?
2. Read Numbers 25:1–13. Why was Phinehas' zeal so impressive?
3. Read 1 Samuel 7:10–13. What does the name 'Ebenezer' mean? Can you think of any other monuments in the Bible set up as reminders to God's people?
4. Read 1 Corinthians 6:9–11. What were the Christians in Corinth supposed to have left behind? Try to come up with a list for today.
5. Read Colossians 3:5. In what ways is covetousness a kind of idolatry?

TO THINK ABOUT AND DISCUSS

1. Which of God's laws are most often ignored or explained away today?
2. Looking back over your own life, are there any events you think are worth commemorating in a way that will be a lasting reminder?
3. Can you think of zealous Christians in church history who have been misunderstood and/or persecuted?
4. Can you think of examples of Christians (past or present) who have shown the wrong kind of zeal, a zeal 'not according to knowledge' (Rom. 10:1–2)?

Part 2
The rules

4 The law

(4:44–6:25)

The Ten Commandments were given 'that it might go well with' Israel (5:29). They lie at the heart of the covenant. While Israel was bound to keep them, more importantly they were bound to the Lord who gave them. Love for him was what the first four commandments were really all about. And love for him was to be their motivation for keeping the other six as well.

Prologue (4:44–5:6)

The introduction to the law begins by stressing *where* it is given—or rather *re*-given. In some ways it is a repetition of the law given at Sinai (or Horeb, as it's referred to throughout Deuteronomy), but much has happened since that initial covenant was entered into. And much is about to happen, too. Entering the land will pose new challenges, bring new dangers and present new opportunities. Repeating the law would be valuable, but in many ways this is an update; a new, improved version[1] tailor-made for a new, improved situation, settled in the land of promise. The location is significant. It is in a valley opposite Beth-peor, with its reminders of Israel's failure, but it is also in the land of Sihon, king of the Amorites, a reminder and pledge of God's faithfulness. The covenant will further reinforce both of those lessons.

The formal introduction to the Ten Commandments makes clear to the people that this is *their* covenant, rather than one made with their fathers (5:3). The events of Sinai were not confined to history, but had given birth to an agreement that is still very much in force. Moses stresses that the covenant is not just something of academic interest from the previous generation. It isn't past its sell-by date: it is current; and that means that it is made with the people in front of Moses every bit as much as it was made with those who were present at Sinai.

The law is to be heard, learned and kept (5:1). The context in which it was initially delivered had made the seriousness of the covenant clear, with the Lord speaking to Moses 'out of the midst of the fire' (5:4). The people had been struck with fear, conscious of the danger of drawing near to such a God (v. 5). Thankfully, they had Moses to stand between the Lord and them as a kind of mediator.

Where did this covenant come from? It was based on the mighty acts of God which had secured Israel's exodus from Egypt and delivered them from slavery. God had done something. The question was, would Israel respond? He had taken the initiative, but would they take hold of this gracious covenant? He was their Redeemer, with every right to command them, but he also had a genuine concern for their welfare. Obedience, then, was the wise, as well as the right, course.

Decalogue (5:7–21)

The law books of most nations are complicated affairs. With Israel it was different. The number of commandments was lower, but the wisdom displayed far greater. A tribal chief among the Toradjas of Indonesia is supposed to have said, 'I would rather have the 7,777 commandments and prohibitions of the Toradja Adat than the 10 commandments of the Christians, for the 10 commandments demand my whole heart, whereas the 7,777 ancestral commands and prohibitions leave room for a lot of freedom.'[2] The God who framed them knows men, women and children inside out, and his commandments have the potential to turn us inside out. The chief was right: they demand the whole heart.

The commandments, as a whole, are designed to ensure that God is given his rightful place in our hearts and lives. And that means us knowing our place, too. The Lord's rightful place is first, and we will have a struggle to put ourselves where we ought to be: last. So the first four (or five[3]) commandments concern our respect for the Lord, his worship, his name and his day. Israel's relationship with the Lord was to be an exclusive one. Polytheism was the norm among the surrounding nations, but *the first commandment* immediately established that things were to be very different in Israel.

> The commandments, as a whole, are designed to ensure that God is given his rightful place in our hearts and lives.

OPENING UP DEUTERONOMY

Each of the gods of the nations was represented in some way in the form of an idol, but *the second commandment* makes clear that worshipping the Lord is a different matter altogether (5:8–10). The character of Israel's God was important, and the different aspects of his character were reflected in his different names. When his 'name' is used in the singular (*third commandment*, v. 11) it usually refers to his whole character. The way we say somebody's name will often give a clear impression of what we think about that person, and it is no different with God's name. If we use the name of the Lord lightly, in an empty ('vain'), meaningless way, it betrays the fact that we have not grasped how weighty his character is. We're supposed to do the opposite—to 'hallow' (i.e. reverence, hold in the highest regard) the name of our heavenly Father.

The fourth commandment (5:12–15) is framed positively—a day of rest (the word 'Sabbath' comes from a root meaning 'to cease/desist') was a wonderful blessing for a people freed from bondage. They could only have dreamed of a day off each week when Pharaoh was their master. It was designed *for* the people, but it was also to be '*to* the Lord' (5:14). That's a difficult balance to strike. We can be confident that we've got it about right when we are able to 'call the Sabbath a delight' (Isa. 58:13).

The next six commandments deal with respect for parents (and authority), life, marriage (and the family), property and the truth. *Commandment number five* (5:16–17) is, as we are reminded in the New Testament (Eph. 6:2), the only one that comes with a promise attached. The importance of this commandment is underlined by the penalty attached to it at the first giving of the law (Deut. 21:18–21). It is clearly fundamental as the assumption is that good parents will use their God-given authority to teach their children to observe the other commandments. Parents are in many ways the most important figures of authority, being the most immediate in society.

The word for 'murder' in *the sixth commandment* (5:17) is not the word usually used for death in war or as a legal punishment. It is not a commandment intended to promote pacifism or outlaw the death penalty. But it is intended to help us recognize that life is a priceless gift from God and that fallen human beings struggle to get on. The example of Cain and Abel, so soon after the fall, is a clear illustration of this. And simple, straightforward murder isn't the only thing that this commandment should caution us against. What our Saviour shows us is that murder has its root in anger (Matt. 5:21–22). We all have a capacity for anger, as well as envy, greed and hatred, which, in a 'perfect storm' of certain circumstances, can turn anyone into a murderer. In a similar way, *the seventh commandment* (5:18) is designed to safeguard marriage, and again the Lord warns us that the act of adultery has its roots in lust (Matt. 5:28). It's a commandment that leaves none of us in a position to throw stones (see John 7:53–8:11).

Commandment number eight (5:19) tells us to respect the property of others. In a world that is on the make and increasingly on the take, this commandment's relevance is apparent. Wheeling and dealing so easily leads us into being economical with the truth, knowingly overpricing, undervaluing, overstating or downplaying, and before we know it we've crossed the line and are stealing.

There's an old story about a baker and a farmer who

fell out over a business arrangement. The baker began to suspect that the farmer was selling him short when he bought pounds of butter. After weighing the slabs of butter on a number of occasions he had the farmer arrested for fraud. The accused farmer, under questioning, admitted that he didn't have a set of weights, so the judge asked him how he could accurately weigh the butter he sold to the baker. 'That's easy,' was the farmer's reply; 'when the baker began to buy from me I decided to buy my bread from him. I've been using his one-pound loaves to balance my scales.'

Commandment nine (5:20) makes clear that the truth, and with it the reputation of others, should also be respected, along with truth in general. The God of the Bible is a God of truth—objective truth—so we shouldn't talk as if it is all relative (i.e. 'your truth' or 'my truth'). Truth matters, and that means that 'white lies' matter too. Even if there is no 'victim' the truth has been a casualty. Our integrity has also been compromised. So the 'little lies' we justify—'Sorry, I had no signal'; 'Yes, you look wonderful in that!'—are important. Straightforward perjury in a court of law is an extreme example, but 'terminological inexactitudes' are located somewhere on a very slippery slope. Christians should be, in Bunyan's phrase, 'Valiant-for-truth', and a half-truth presented as the whole truth is an untruth.

The final commandment (5:21) is a bit different.

If you see something that someone else has,
And think to yourself that you'd love it,
The Bible will tell you, you'd better beware,
In your heart you're beginning to covet!

OPENING UP DEUTERONOMY

This concerns our hearts and uncovers where breaches of the other commandments spring from. Instead of dealing with the symptoms, it goes to the source. It certainly exposed the heart of Saul of Tarsus, as he tells us in his letter to the Christians in Rome. The young 'Pharisee, a son of Pharisees' (Acts 23:6) was untroubled by the first nine 'words', convinced that he was keeping them. But with the tenth it was another story. When Saul read the tenth commandment, 'sin, seizing an opportunity through the commandment, produced in me all kinds of covetousness' (Rom. 7:8). The result? 'I died,' says Paul. All hopes of attaining righteousness through the keeping of the law foundered on the final commandment. No wonder the apostle came to love talking about being 'justified by faith in Christ and not by works of the law' (Gal. 2:16).

Of course, the other commandments, rightly understood, were also supposed to reach the heart, as Jesus shows us in the way he applies them in the Sermon on the Mount. In short, the law condemns us all, even top Pharisees. If we've listened carefully to the law we should be like the man who was on trial and pleading 'not guilty'. At the end of the first day in court he changed his plea to 'guilty'. 'Why didn't you admit it earlier?' asked the judge. 'Well, I didn't realize I was guilty until I had heard all the evidence,' came the reply.

Epilogue (5:22–6:25)

Israel's response to the commandments was a strange mixture of fear and self-confidence (5:22–27). The fear associated with being in the presence of a holy God was natural. Some of the godliest men of the Old Testament (e.g. Job, Isaiah and Daniel), along with the disciples of the New (e.g. Peter and John), exhibit this instinctive reaction. Coupled with this, however, was a lack of appreciation of just how difficult keeping these laws would prove to be. There is a right kind of fear that is closely linked with keeping God's commandments, but it all depends on the state of the heart. The law is good (as Paul affirms—Rom. 7:12). The problem is that we aren't. Our hearts are hard (Matt. 19:8; Eph. 4:18), deceitful (Jer. 17:9), and with a bias towards disobedience. We will find ourselves having to take frequent corrective action if we are to keep to this path that the commandments lay before us.

> The law is good. The problem is that we aren't.

The fear we need is what has been referred to as 'filial fear'—the fear of offending a Father we respect greatly and love deeply. Following his commands won't get us into trouble (ultimately!), but will simply secure blessings. There are ten commandments, but only one Lord. Love for him will help us with all the commandments because we will want to please him. While orthodox Jews have taken literally the references to hands, eyes, doorposts and gates (6:8), the real meaning is that our lives should revolve around the commandments. Having the law about your person (on your mobile?) or around the house (a framed text on the mantelpiece?) is no substitute for having it in your heart.

A second reciting of the law was especially necessary because life in the land of promise would have particular dangers. Having everything served up for them on a plate, as it were, would introduce the dangerous possibility of feeling self-sufficient. They had faced very different temptations in the wilderness, but in many ways prosperity and plenty would prove to be a bigger test than the challenges of the desert. In such circumstances it would be frighteningly easy to forget God. And then it would be just a short step to 'go after other gods' (6:14)—a step with grave consequences. They had put their God to the test at Massah (6:16), questioning whether the Lord was really with them when they were hungry. They would, in effect, be making the same mistake again—failing to acknowledge the Lord's presence—by forgetting him in the midst of plenty. A diligent keeping of the commandments, in contrast, would have much happier results.

At the end of chapter 6 we are alerted to the fact that carefully keeping 'all this commandment' is a way of attaining 'righteousness' (6:25). Sadly, a 100 per cent score would prove to be beyond Israel (and everyone else!). Still, there is a relative righteousness that we do well to seek after. What the New Testament will warn us again and again is not to think that this is a way to be saved. It's the way to live, but not the way to eternal life. It's what the people of God should become, but not the way to become one of the people of God. For that we depend upon the righteousness—the perfect righteousness—of another. The impeccable life of Jesus Christ can be reckoned as ours, put to our account. But only by faith: *not* by works.

FOR FURTHER STUDY

1. Find clear (and preferably well-known) biblical examples of someone breaking each of the Ten Commandments.
2. Can you think of some more subtle breaches of each commandment?
3. Read Jeremiah 31:31–34 and Ezekiel 37:21–28. What do these passages have to say about obedience under the new covenant?
4. Read Luke 18:18–27. Which commandment does Jesus miss out initially, and why? Why don't we apply Jesus' command literally to every Christian?
5. Read Colossians 2:16–17. Do some research to find out why many Bible-believing Christians don't think this verse applies to the Lord's Day. What other reasons are there to conclude that the fourth commandment still applies to Christians?

TO THINK ABOUT AND DISCUSS

1. What would you say to someone who asked why Sunday is special to Christians? How many benefits can you think of that come from carefully observing the Lord's Day?
2. What are the particular dangers for Christians living in the twenty-first century where you are?
3. Has there been a time when you have suddenly recognized that one of the Ten Commandments applied to a situation in your own life that you hadn't seen before?
4. Can you think of any times when difficulties have done you spiritual good?
5. What, apart from obedience, do you think is involved in 'honouring' parents?
6. What would you say to someone advocating abortion? Suicide? Euthanasia?
7. How many common and generally accepted ways of stealing can you think of (e.g. watering-down drinks, illegal photocopying, plagiarism)?

5 Commandment one: the devotion principle

(7:1–11:32)

In these chapters Moses paints three pictures. One is of the past, and it's not pretty. Then he portrays two possible futures for Israel: blessing or curse. There is one big lesson running through these chapters: 'Don't be stubborn. Do be obedient.'

The devotion principle

The first commandment comes first for a reason. The God of Israel is, as we have seen, the one and only God. That means there is no room for any other so-called 'gods'. From our perspective that seems fairly obvious, but in those days it was virtually unheard of to demand exclusive worship. It was standard practice to adopt a variety of gods who demanded devotion of a particular kind and promised specific blessings in return. You could take a pick-and-mix approach depending on your own requirements. Different gods could help in different ways, much like the (unbiblical) idea of patron saints within Roman Catholicism.

It would be very easy for Israel to adopt a form of syncretism on entering the land, worshipping the Lord but with a place for Canaanite gods alongside. This was a real threat, and it explains why Israel were to have 'no other gods before' the Lord. The top priority for Israel on entering the promised land was to ensure that they dealt ruthlessly with the Canaanites. In our soft age this can sound very harsh, so it's worth reminding ourselves that the Canaanites were guilty of many abominations (7:25–26; 12:31; 13:14; 17:1, 4; 18:12; 22:5; 23:18; 25:16; 27:15) and so were subject to the just judgement of God. The Israelites were merely the instrument the Lord used to carry out his sentence. At other times in history he would use other nations to visit judgements on his own people, so there was no special treatment for Israel.

Devoted to destruction (7:1–5)

The ruthlessness was necessary because of the danger these people posed. To have more than one god was to have divided loyalties instead of wholehearted devotion. Any temptation to 'serve other gods' (v. 4) is seen as a kind of infectious disease which Israel needs to steer clear of at all costs. There can be no compromise, no covenant, no mercy and no intermarriage, because there must be no turning away from the only true God. Altars and pillars must be decisively and comprehensively dealt with (v. 5).

Devoted to obedience (7:6–11)

The Canaanites had been devoted to idolatry, and now are to

be devoted to destruction. Israel, though, are to be devoted to the Lord. He has chosen them, and they need to choose, and keep on choosing, the Lord—just as we do. The word 'holy' literally means 'separate' and has two aspects: who they are to be separated *from* and who they are to be separated *to*. Israel are his treasured possession, and they ought to treasure him. It would do them good to remember their humble beginnings and be aware that they owe their current strength in numbers to the love and faithfulness of the Lord. The love shown and the oath sworn to their fathers came out of nowhere—it was pure grace.[1] While totally unexpected and undeserved, it came from a faithful, covenant-keeping God. It was no short-term arrangement but had the potential to bless 'a thousand generations' (v. 9). Those hard-hearted enough to hate such a good God would be repaid with destruction.

Remember Pharaoh and be fearless (7:12–26)

Those careful in their keeping of the Lord's commands would enjoy the love of the Lord expressed to them in concrete ways. A variety of blessings are mentioned, all associated with fruitfulness of one kind or another and protection from disease. As well as blessings of the field, they are also promised blessings on the battlefield. It's a promise that requires Israel's trust coupled with a refusal to give way to fear. A good memory will come in handy. All they need to do when things look bleak is to 'remember what the LORD [their] God did to Pharaoh' (v. 18). Their confidence is to be firmly placed in the Lord of plagues and Passover. He will ensure the ultimate destruction of their enemies.[2] What they need to do is to ensure that they destroy 'the carved images of their [the

Canaanites'] gods' (v. 25). Failure to do so will mean their own destruction instead. The real danger comes not from their enemies' military prowess, but from the attraction of their silver and gold.

Remember the way and be humble (8:1–20)

There is something else they would do well to remember: the way they have been led. It was a lesson in humility, the chief ingredients of which were dependence and discipline. They learned to depend upon God in the wilderness for their food, clothing and strength. It is a lesson they could easily forget once they are settled in a land in which they will 'lack nothing' (v. 9). It is important that as they eat their fill they thank the Lord and their hearts are humbled at his goodness towards them. Otherwise the likelihood is that their hearts will be 'lifted up' (v. 14) and the Lord will be forgotten altogether. It would be so easy to take the credit themselves for all that they have accomplished and acquired. 'I've worked hard to get to where I am, and I'm proud of myself' is a popular perspective among the successful. 'I owe it all to the Lord; without him I wouldn't be where I am today' is a less common attitude. And then there is the danger of saying the right thing while our hearts are nevertheless 'lifted up'.

Hopefully the discipline that they received during their wanderings will make them think twice before ignoring the Lord's solemn warnings. If not, they will suffer the same fate as the nations they are about to dispossess.

Remember who's with you and be fearless (9:1–3)

While there are things they need to remember from the past,

what they know in the present will prove no less important once they have crossed the Jordan (9:1). Moses' pep talk is rooted in reality. He doesn't pretend that the task will be easy. Many of today's motivational speakers would consider it a mistake to mention the might of their enemies, the strength of the cities' fortifications and the height of the Anakim (vv. 1–2). But knowing who is going before them 'as a consuming fire' (v. 3) will be all they need to put these obstacles into perspective. Again, though, this is only half the battle. After victory they could undo all their good work by drawing the wrong conclusions. They could infer that the blessings they are enjoying have been earned rather than received as a gift. Big mistake! There were only two real reasons why Israel would gain possession of the land—because the nations had forfeited it, and the Lord had promised it.

> Moses' pep talk is rooted in reality. He doesn't pretend that the task will be easy.

Remember your provocations and be humble (9:4–12)

Gentile wickedness rather than Jewish righteousness is the explanation for the blessings they are to enjoy. Here is something else Israel need to remember and know: they have been, and are, stubborn. The journey from Egypt to the Jordan was a story of one provocation after another. As Moses was receiving the tablets of stone the people were demonstrating how quickly they could 'turn aside … out of the way' (see Exod. 32:8). And the rest of their history has showed how slow they are to turn back to the right way.

The golden calf was clearly the lowest point, but it was the worst of many low points. Israel have no grounds for pride. They should be humbled by the Lord's goodness to them, not 'lifted up'.

Remember Moses' intercession and fear the Lord (9:13–10:11)

They could also learn from Moses' intercession for them each time they strayed from the straight and narrow. Three times in this section Moses speaks of how his prayers had averted disaster (9:18–19; 9:25–29; 10:10). Far from their having been righteous, Moses had to pray for them that the Lord would 'not regard' their 'stubbornness … or their wickedness or their sin' (9:27). His prevailing plea wasn't based on anything to do with Israel. The Lord's promise to Abraham, Isaac and Jacob meant that his honour was at stake. There was also the concern that Egypt might draw God-dishonouring conclusions from Israel's destruction, accusing their God of being either powerless or loveless.

Two other reminders should help Israel as they go forward. The second set of tablets, Moses says, are at that very moment in the ark—a permanent reminder of Israel's waywardness (in needing a second set) and of the commandments themselves. The tribe of Levi will also be a living reminder to the nation that, just as the Lord was Levi's inheritance in a literal way, the same should be true of Israel as a whole in a spiritual sense.

Remember what's required and circumcise your hearts (10:12–11:1)

Having gone over all the times when Israel got it wrong, it's a good time to sum up what getting things right will look like.

Moses uses four verbs to express Israel's duty to the Lord who has been so gracious to them: fear, walk, love and serve. Two words concern their attitude to God and two describe their conduct. Fear and love sound like a rather odd couple, but not if we understand the fear to be that 'deep reverence and awe' we mentioned in Chapter 4. A love that fears to offend and desires to please is something we can all understand. To walk in God's ways and to serve him are a more obvious pair. To walk in his ways *is* to serve him—though it needs to be 'all' his ways, just as the service needs to be what we would call 'wholehearted'. It's not an unreasonable requirement from the one who has set his heart on this people. The steadfast love of the Lord certainly isn't half-hearted. But we have a heart problem—sometimes referred to as being hard-hearted and here called stubbornness (10:16).

The opposite of this is to have a 'circumcised' heart. We have a responsibility here. In one place the Lord is clearly said to be the one who needs to circumcise our hearts (30:6), but here and elsewhere we are told to do the circumcising (10:16; Jer. 4:4). The picture of circumcision is a difficult one for us to appreciate, but in essence the Lord is telling us to open our hearts to him—although we need to be aware that we won't manage it in our own strength without the Lord's help. Something else that will help us, though, is to recall to our minds (in a way calculated to affect our hearts) who it is we're serving and what he has done for us (10:17–22). The way he looked after Israel in the wilderness was to be a model for Israel's treatment of 'sojourners' in their midst (10:19)—a principle that lies behind a number of specific laws that crop up later in Deuteronomy. It should help them to be loving to others, but also to love the Lord their God. It is a love to be expressed in obedience—not a soppy sentimental thing, but not a cold, clinical, rule-keeping exercise either. His commandments were never supposed to be burdensome (1 John 5:3).

Remember the Lord's discipline and be obedient (11:2–32)

Another motivation for Israel is to remember the kind of discipline they could expect if they proved disobedient. What was experienced by Pharaoh at the Red Sea, by Israel in the wilderness, and by Dathan and Abiram when they rebelled against Moses (vv. 2–7) ought to have a sobering effect on anyone. But Israel are not to lose sight of the promises. The blessings in store for the obedient are recited once again, alongside the promised care of a generous God. But there is an ever-present danger—idolatry—which will anger their loving Lord and lead to disaster.

These commandments couldn't be more important, and the choice couldn't be more stark. Mount Gerizim and Mount Ebal (v. 29) serve as visual aids to enforce the simple truth that there are two paths, one blessed and the other accursed. The choice is theirs.

For further study ▶

FOR FURTHER STUDY

1. What other nations were used by God in the Old Testament as instruments of judgement on his own people?
2. Read Matthew 5:27–30. While Jesus clearly doesn't expect to be taken literally, we must take his words seriously. What might need to be 'torn out' or 'cut off' in contemporary Christian living?
3. Read Psalms 78; 105; 136. How would these psalms help Israel to recall who God is and what he had done for them? What do they focus on? What might a Christian add?
4. Read Hebrews 12:3–11. What encouragements and advice does this passage give us for when we are being disciplined?

TO THINK ABOUT AND DISCUSS

1. What do you find humbling as you review the way that you have been led?
2. What kinds of things most commonly leave people's hearts 'lifted up' today?
3. What is especially difficult about the task facing the church and the individual Christian today?
4. Can you think of times when you have been foolishly stubborn? What might have helped you at the time?
5. What forms of discipline do we see the Lord using in the Bible? What kinds of discipline do you think you have experienced?

6 Commandments two to four

(12:1–16:17)

Having established that the Lord alone is God, the next three commandments tell us how to worship him in the right place, in the right way and at the right times. Israel would need to steer clear of anything associated with other so-called gods and stick to the Lord's blueprint.

Commandment two: the worship principle (12:1–13:18)

The second commandment immediately alerts us to the fact that there is a wrong way to worship the Lord. That is why Canaan is to be stripped of its altars and images. There is no place for images in Israel's worship, and only one designated place of worship. The way to worship God isn't left up to us. We don't get to choose—the Lord has chosen. It's not about what pleases us, but about what pleases him. As New Testament Christians the place no longer matters, but the way we worship emphatically does. 'In spirit and truth' (John 4:23–24) is the kind of worship the Lord is looking for.

The freedom of the promised land does not mean that Israel are free to do what they like when it comes to worship. The people still need to be careful not to eat the blood of any animals slaughtered for food. Tithes, firstborn and vow offerings all need to be brought to the chosen place of worship.

Further safeguards follow to keep the people from idolatry. They aren't even to *ask* about the foreign gods of the Canaanites (12:30). It could so easily be the start of a slippery slope leading to abominations like child sacrifice. Nor are they to listen to anybody advocating the worship of other gods, even if the message is accompanied with 'a sign or wonder' (13:1–3). However plausible such a person might seem, such advice should be considered a test from the Lord as to whether Israel will stick to their guns or cave in to peer pressure. Such teaching is no innocent mistake but an act of rebellion. What will be Israel's greatest safeguard against being led astray? Love for the Lord. In a marriage, it is when love has grown cold that the wife or husband is most vulnerable to advances from the opposite sex. It's the same in our relationship with God. Where our love for him is 'with all [our] heart and with all [our] soul' (13:3), we will 'hold fast' to him.

To lead the people away from God would be an act of high treason, deserving of the ultimate punishment. The book of Deuteronomy unashamedly prescribes the death sentence a number of times. From Genesis onwards (Gen. 9:5–6) the Bible makes clear that certain sins committed wilfully mean that the offender forfeits his or her right to life. While we would perhaps hesitate to make that call ourselves, when the Word of God tells us that something is that serious, we need to take it on board. A number of deaths occur in the Bible simply because people didn't take seriously warnings that spelled out the consequences of specific offences. It all began back in the garden of Eden when the serpent said, 'You will not surely die' (Gen. 3:4). We believe his lies at our peril. Such pernicious influences need to be 'purged'. We might initially think that a doctor is being too radical if he wants us to go into surgery without delay to have a tumour removed; but he knows what will happen if action isn't taken immediately. Nobody would accuse a doctor of being harsh in a situation like that—we assume that he knows what he's doing. It is safe to assume that the Lord has far greater wisdom and love, and when the penalty seems harsh, there is a very good reason for it.

The Lord Jesus warned us to 'hate [our] own father and mother ... and brothers and sisters' (Luke 14:26) in comparison to him, and in the scenario Moses is dealing with here, being related to the offender shouldn't change anything (13:6–8). Care needs to be taken to establish the facts before such a solemn sentence is carried out—as Moses points out; but whether it is a close relative or a whole city there can be no exceptions.

Commandment three: the holiness principle (14:1–29)

This section's connection with the third commandment may not be immediately apparent, but it becomes much clearer when we appreciate what 'taking the name of the LORD' really involves. The Hebrew word translated 'take' means 'to bear or carry' in a sense not confined to our speech, and 'the name of the LORD' is used as a kind of shorthand for the character or reputation of God. While the commandment would include verbally misusing the name of God, its application is far broader. The Lord's people bear the Lord's name, and that means they should live in a way consistent with that fact; otherwise the claim to belong to him is an empty one, made in vain. So this section deals with a number of practices that would amount to a denial of Israel's exclusive relationship with the Lord their God.

> The Lord's people bear the Lord's name, and that means they should live in a way consistent with that fact; otherwise the claim to belong to him is an empty one, made in vain.

The prohibition of cutting or making baldness on the forehead (v. 1) is a reference to practices associated with Canaanite religion, as the phrase 'for the dead' indicates. The cutting was probably considered a mark of ownership, as the reason given for not following this practice—that they are a 'people holy to the LORD'—seems to suggest.

The distinction between clean and unclean animals (vv. 3–21) has been the subject of much debate. There may well be an element of health and hygiene lying behind the rules laid down. It also looks as if unusual animals—those that in some way seem to be an 'unnatural' mixture of features—are categorized as unclean. If that is so, the message to avoid getting 'mixed up' with what is contrary to the laws of God (natural here, as well as moral) is being reinforced. Others have argued that the distinctions are quite arbitrary and that is the point—it is just a test of obedience, for obedience' sake. Israel would learn that the whole of their daily life needed to revolve around distinguishing between the clean and the unclean, much as the Christian's life should be concerned with 'discerning' the good and perfect will of God (Rom. 12:2) as opposed to the influences of the world, the flesh and the devil. Whatever the full significance of the dietary laws, it is being 'a people holy to the LORD' that makes observing them so important. The New Testament employs the same motivation time and again for consistent Christian living. We are the Lord's, and we need to live accordingly (Eph. 4:1; Phil. 1:27).

The closing command to not boil 'a young goat in its mother's milk' (v. 21) is thought to be a reference to an ancient fertility rite practised in Canaan.

While there can be no compromise when it comes to some laws, there is a good deal more latitude allowed with regard to others. The Lord 'knows our frame, and he remembers that we are dust' (Ps. 103:14), and he recognizes some of the situations where sticking to the letter of the law will prove needlessly difficult. Regarding tithes, provision is made for those living a long way off. The principle that the tithe must be brought to the assigned place of worship is maintained, but permission is granted to convert the tithe into money and then to change it back into produce. The aim of these regulations is to help the people 'learn to fear the LORD their God' (v. 23), and the link with the third commandment is underlined by twice mentioning that the designated place of worship is where the Lord's name resides (vv. 23–24).

A couple of reminders of their obligation to look after the Levites are inserted here as well (vv. 27, 29). Deep respect for the Lord will mean a deep concern for those who minister before the Lord on behalf of the people. The priests represent the Lord in a special way, and are 'a people holy to the Lord' (v. 2) in a special sense. They are a unique, living illustration of what it means to bear the Lord's name in a meaningful, worthy manner (the opposite of taking it in vain). They should be valued because of their special God-given role. 'The sojourner, the fatherless, and the widow' (v. 29) should also be cared for, because the Lord cares for them.

Commandment four: the Sabbath principle (15:1–16:17)

The Sabbath day had been firmly established at Mount Sinai and observed throughout the wilderness wanderings. With Israel looking ahead to life in the land of Canaan, the similar principle of a Sabbath year is outlined. The year of release was a provision for any who fell on hard times, giving them an opportunity to get back on their feet. It was a law that was needed because it is human nature to take advantage of the weakness of others for our own profit. That is not to say that we aren't capable of acts of generosity, but, in national terms, they are few and far between. All too often our 'good deeds' come when it suits us, when they have a feel-good factor attached, or with the hope that they will help us feel less guilty. The poor and weak need protection in law, and the Lord ensured that in Israel they got it. Even with safeguards like these, however, the human heart has a way of finding loopholes, and Moses warns against the 'unworthy thought' (15:9) that is likely to arise when the year of release draws near. By then there will be little time for the repaying of any loans before they are wiped out in the seventh year. The Lord 'loves a cheerful giver' (2 Cor. 9:7), but left to ourselves, 'grudging' is usually the adjective that applies. Liberality (generosity, 15:14) is the goal.

The Lord has given them much—not least their freedom. That means they should be slow to enslave others and ready to grant freedom. Remembering their own struggles in Egypt should soften their hearts towards others in difficulty. The words 'It shall not seem hard to you' (15:18) alert us to the danger that a situation like that is likely to seem hard. Feeling 'hard done by' comes easily to us. Recognizing all the reasons we have to be thankful is a more difficult proposition.

Firstborn males among their herds and flocks are to be dedicated to the Lord (15:19) and eaten at the place of worship, except for those with some kind of blemish. A sacrifice, to be acceptable to God, must be spotless and whole, just like the ultimate sacrifice that it foreshadows.

The appointed place of worship is to become the nation's focal point three times each year. The feasts of Passover, Weeks and Booths are to bring all the men of Israel together 'before the LORD' (16:16). Passover was a time to remember the exodus from Egypt, with a practical application attached. The removal of all leaven is symbolic of the purging of sin from their midst—the right response to God's glorious deliverance.

The Feast of Weeks is to be a celebration, fifty days (indicating a kind of jubilee) after Passover, marking the beginning of harvest. We know from the New Testament that this looked forward to the beginning of a different kind of harvest on the day of Pentecost (meaning 'fifty'). Not for the first time, they are reminded of their slavery in Egypt as a motivation for showing compassion to their servants, along with others who depend on the care of others (the Levites, foreigners, the fatherless and widows, 16:11–12).

The Feast of Booths is another celebration of the Lord's goodness which comes once the harvest has been gathered in (16:13). It is an acknowledgement that every grain and grape is a blessing from God.

While all three feasts are times of thanksgiving, they are also to be times of giving. 'Appear[ing] before the LORD empty-handed' is not an option (16:16). The amount is not specified, but the principle is clear: 'as he is able' (16:17). It is a principle that applies to us today, as Paul explains to the Christians at Corinth (2 Cor. 8:12). Whatever we are able to give is only 'according to the blessing of the LORD [our] God' that we have received (Deut. 16:17). David recognized this when the people came with their offerings for the building of the temple: 'O LORD our God, all this abundance that we have provided for building you a house for your holy name comes from your hand and is all your own' (1 Chr. 29:16). The question is not to be, 'How much shall I give?' but rather, 'How much shall I keep?'

FOR FURTHER STUDY

1. Read John 4:19–24. What do the Lord's words here tell us about how we should view church buildings and New Testament worship?
2. How many deaths in the Bible can you think of that came about as a result of ignoring clear warnings?
3. Read 2 Corinthians 8:1–15; 9:6–7. What biblical principles for giving can we glean from these verses?
4. Read 1 Corinthians 11:23–29. What particular truths does the New Testament feast of the Lord's Supper focus our minds on? What should be our approach to it? What do you think should be the prevailing mood?

TO THINK ABOUT AND DISCUSS

1. What would you say to someone who asked you whether Christians today should tithe?
2. When was the last time you were generous? What was your main motivation?
3. How many bad reasons for doing 'good works' can you think of, and which are the most common?
4. What is the origin of the practice of 'saying grace' before meals? Is it biblical? How might it be helpful, and what potential drawbacks to the practice can you see?

7 Commandments five and six

(16:18–22:8)

When Israel enter the promised land they will need to apply the fifth and sixth commandments to their new situation. Respect for those in positions of authority and an understanding of the sanctity of life will be guiding principles for the new nation. This is a section laced with warnings and punctuated by promises that speak to us too.

The fifth commandment: the authority principle (16:18–18:22)

The focus now moves away from 'the place that the Lord will choose' (16:15) for Israel's worship to the civil government of the nation. Moses is taking the theme of the fifth commandment and applying it to the new situation Israel are soon to confront. The authority of parents is clearly stated in the original 'ten words', but the principle of God-given authority extends beyond families to nations. Moses won't be around to settle disputes once they are in the promised land. There will need to be 'judges and officers' in all the towns of Israel (16:18). But not any old person will do. If justice is to be upheld, impartiality among those in authority will be essential. Man hasn't changed over the centuries. Those with influence are always vulnerable to offers of bribes. 'Every man has his price' is a proverb too close to the truth for comfort. It was to Luther's credit (and the pope's confusion) that he could not be silenced by the offer of a cardinal's hat. In the book of Acts we learn that Felix, the governor of Judea, was hoping for a bribe (Acts 24:26). Power corrupts, and many countries in the world today struggle because corruption is endemic throughout many of their institutions. Law and order inevitably break down when there is no confidence in the judiciary and/or the judicial system. Justice was to be the cornerstone of the new nation once settled in the land. For centuries the Lord would raise up prophets to denounce Israel and its leaders when they failed to judge 'with righteous judgement' (16:18; see John 7:24).

The authorities in Israel are to be on the lookout for the first signs of idolatrous or sub-standard worship. The civil penalty for such offences is stated, along with some safeguards to be part of the legal process. First of all, care has to be taken to establish the facts; there is to be no rush to judgement. Secondly, two or three witnesses are required, who are to take a leading role in carrying out the sentence—even a dulled conscience is likely to have qualms about making false accusations that will involve them in murder. Finally, there is to be a final court of appeal, consisting of Levitical priests and an appointed judge, for difficult cases. That these appeals are to take place, and the sentence delivered, at the appointed place of worship makes it abundantly clear that the ultimate authority behind the decision is the Lord's. Twice we're reminded that the goal of law enforcement is to purge evil from Israel's midst (17:7, 12).

The laws of Israel don't apply to nations now, but churches have a similar responsibility to govern themselves in a way that is just.

The next set of laws reminds us that the Lawgiver not only knows human nature, but he also knows the future. Another kind of authority will one day be part of the nation and the Lord, through Moses, makes provision for that eventuality. Israel will ultimately end up with kings (17:14–20), and they will need to be especially careful. Horses (the status symbol of the day, and also a measure of military strength), wives, silver and gold could all be their downfall. Not only would acquiring horses involve a literal return to Egypt, but all these pitfalls would be a kind of spiritual return to Egypt in so far as they are representative of worldliness in general. Wives have unique access to, and influence over, the hearts of their husbands. The sad fact is that a wife can turn a husband's heart away from God. Many have ignored this warning to their own hurt. Even the wisdom of Solomon may not be enough to protect you from making this mistake (1 Kings 11:1–4)!

The deceitfulness of riches is hard to overstate. Our Lord had a surprising amount to say about money. It's another area where those in authority will need to take particular care. For a king, with everyone fearing him, the temptation would be to forget that he was answerable to a higher authority. To fear the Lord, though, is even more important for kings than for commoners if they are to rule well. And there is another danger: when we stop looking up to God, it won't be long before we start looking down on others (17:20). Just as Israel's enjoyment of the land depended on their obedience, so did the king and his descendants' occupation of the throne.

As well as the chosen place for worship and the chosen king to rule, there are also instructions for

> When we stop looking up to God, it won't be long before we start looking down on others.

the chosen tribe of Levi (18:1–8). They have been chosen 'to stand and minister in the name of the LORD' (18:5) on behalf of the people. As they dedicate themselves to their calling, the people have a responsibility to provide for them.

Next comes a warning about the potentially disastrous influence of false priests like those who hold sway over the minds of Canaan's current inhabitants. We have already seen that the Lord was driving the nations out of the land because of their wickedness, and here Israel are warned about some of their 'abominations' (18:9–14). On no account are Israel to adopt any of these occult practices. Fortune-tellers and diviners (18:14) are to have no place in the life of the nation. Israel are to be different. If they follow the example of the nations they will, in the end, suffer the same fate as the nations. Imposters are not to be listened to.

Moses promises that one day the Lord will raise up a prophet that Israel will need to listen to (18:15). True prophets mediated God's word to the people and were to be heeded accordingly. False prophets, on the other hand, would forfeit their lives: it is a serious matter to claim to speak with divine authority (see Gal. 1:6–9). Such people often gain their influence because people are too afraid to challenge them, but just one concrete example of their speaking falsely will be enough to establish their deception. Then it will be their turn to fear, not the people's. The immediate fulfilment of this promise may well be the prophet Samuel, and we can see further fulfilments in the long line of true prophets that the Lord raised up to call Israel back from their wicked ways. The Jews, however, looked for a final prophet who would fill this role. Such an expectation lay behind some of the theories regarding Jesus of Nazareth (e.g. John 1:21) and gives added significance to the words spoken from heaven at his transfiguration ('listen to him', Matt. 17:5). Jesus is the prophet above all other prophets that both Jews and Gentiles should listen to carefully. Peter was in no doubt that Jesus is the prophet spoken of here—the one they'd all been waiting for (Acts 3:22–23).

> **Jesus is the prophet above all other prophets that both Jews and Gentiles should listen to carefully.**

The sixth commandment: the life principle (19:1–22:8)

'You shall not murder' is, as commandments go, pretty straightforward. But often the circumstances surrounding a 'murder' are anything but straightforward. The cities of refuge are another merciful 'provision' (19:4) that recognizes the difference between murder and manslaughter. The guilt of taking another life had to be treated seriously, but where it was unintentional—an accident that is part of being in a fallen world—it could also be treated mercifully. The danger of family feuds was a particularly real one in those times, and they could last for generations. It was generally considered fair for a victim's family to avenge the blood of their loved one, meaning that situations could quickly escalate. Three cities of refuge had already been established east of the Jordan, and now three more were to be designated in the promised land itself. They were to be spaced out across the country to ensure that one was accessible wherever you were. No premeditating murderer could expect to find refuge, though.

A single verse deals with the importance of respecting (rather than moving) property boundaries (19:14), presumably because this was likely to be the cause of many disputes, some potentially involving murder. That would explain why, as the penalty for maliciously bringing a false accusation is outlined, the first phrase used is 'life for life' (19:21).

It is in this context that the 'eye for eye, tooth for tooth' principle is introduced to determine the correct punishment. It is not a principle to apply in relationships, but for legal situations where false accusations are made. The Lord Jesus has made clear that this is no rule of thumb for the Christian (Matt. 5:38–42). If the false accuser had hoped to secure the death penalty for the accused, that is what he himself must face, with the exact equivalent being the sentence in every case. This is clearly an appropriate and proportionate punishment designed to ensure that legal disputes did not degenerate into personal vendettas, and to maintain the integrity of the system as a whole. What better way to make people think twice before using the law courts to settle grudges?

Entering the promised land meant entering a theatre of war, so battle guidelines come as no surprise (20:1–20). The first rule is a striking one: no fear allowed! And it is backed up with a reason: 'the LORD your God is with you' (20:1, 4). Not too many army manuals would encourage officers to remind their men that death is a real possibility on the day of battle, but then the people of God can afford to be realistic. Anything that might weaken an individual's resolve, and thus army morale in general, is considered grounds for a discharge; even fear itself counts.

The word 'murder' used in the sixth commandment is not the usual one used in Hebrew to describe killing in war. That is altogether different. Nevertheless, there are rules that Israel need to follow to ensure that they aren't guilty of murder as they fight their enemies. A distinction is drawn between distant cities and those that are near, permitting both plunder and mercy in the former, but neither in the latter. The danger of learning the people's wicked ways is too great to think about sparing any. A scorched-earth policy, though, is also out of the question. Trees that the Lord has provided for food are to be preserved, and eating of their fruit is permitted (20:19–20).

Even in time of war the taking of life is such a serious business that when the murderer is not known there is a kind of 'blood guilt' that has to be atoned for by the elders of the nearest city (21:3). A law giving rights to captured women (21:10–14) would have been unheard of in those days, but the people of God needed to learn that, just because they were at war, and just because they won, it didn't mean they could do what they liked. The shaving of the head and paring of the nails are outward symbols of mourning allowing the woman to grieve (21:12). Today we might describe this in terms of 'closure'—an opportunity to come to terms with what has happened and to prepare for a new chapter in life.

The rights of the firstborn son, even if he is the son of an unloved second wife, are legally protected (21:15–17), and the family unit is safeguarded by what we might consider a draconian law concerning obedience (21:18–21). Honouring parents made the top ten, of course, so we shouldn't be too surprised that its importance is underlined with a death sentence. That it hits us so hard tells us just how much our modern view of things differs from the Bible on this point.

Also thrown in here is a law that seems unimportant unless we are reading Deuteronomy in light of the New Testament. Who would have thought that an obscure law about execution (21:22–23) would take on such huge significance? Here the concern is the defiling of the land. We have already seen the importance of purging, but there is also the danger of defiling. To be hanged was to be 'cursed by God' (21:23). A man who was 'undefiled' (or 'unstained', Heb. 7:26) would one day hang on a tree, made a curse for us, so that we might be blessed.

Respect for the property of others, and an attitude of looking out for one another, are stressed in the next law (22:1–4). We can't just say, 'That's not my responsibility'; Israel were to be a community quick to help one another, just as the church is to be today.

Cross-dressing isn't an innocent bit of experimentation, according to the Bible (22:5); it is an 'abomination' that is contrary to nature, though there may be the added factor of a connection with Canaanite religious practices.

The law allowing the taking of young birds but stipulating the leaving of the mother (22:6–7) parallels the law about fruit trees in a siege. It was important not to be greedy and not only to think about the short term. The continuing life cycle of nature was to be preserved. This whole idea of 'sustainability' has a very modern ring to it. Our environment, our farmers and our fishermen would be in a much better position if this principle had been applied in their particular areas.

The command to make parapets for every roof is also very up to date (22:8). Health and safety legislation can sometimes be ridiculous in its unrealistic detail, but the whole concept of 'a duty of care' dates right back to Moses. Life—whether in the form of trees, animals or humans—is precious.

FOR FURTHER STUDY

1. Read James 2:1–9. What sort of 'evil thoughts' do you think James has in mind? What is James saying is so wrong with partiality?
2. Read 1 Corinthians 5:3–13. How does Paul apply the principle of 'purging'? Why do you think he restricts the responsibility of purging to 'inside the church', and what are the implications?
3. Read 2 Corinthians 6:14–7:1. What sort of 'yoking' does Paul have in mind here? Can this principle be applied to other areas?
4. See how many times you can find the phrase 'one another' used in the book of Acts.
5. Read Matthew 7:15–20. Jesus makes 'fruit' the key in identifying false prophets. By looking at other New Testament warnings about false prophets, draw up a list of the kind of fruit we would expect to see.

TO THINK ABOUT AND DISCUSS

1. What are the signs of sub-standard worship that we should be on the lookout for today?
2. What kinds of partiality are still a problem in churches?
3. What authorities should we all be subject to? Why do you think we find it so hard and tend to rebel against authority figures?
4. Horses may not be a problem, but what are the big temptations for you in your situation?
5. Can you think of any news stories or incidents in your own life that illustrate the importance of establishing the facts of a situation before acting?
6. Do you think the church today is good at fulfilling its responsibility to provide financially for those who minister God's Word?
7. What do you think might count as common 'abominations' in the Western world today?

8 Commandments seven to ten

(22:9–26:19)

Commandments seven to ten also have particular applications for Israel in their land. Purity, property and justice need to be guarded, while contentment and commitment are to be nurtured.

The seventh commandment: the purity principle (22:9–23:14)

Laws stressing the importance of avoiding the mixing of crops, animals and materials (22:9–12) are probably a kind of symbolic reinforcing of the warnings about 'mixing' with the pagan people and practices of Canaan. Purity is a concept that Israel need to grasp. Sexual purity is the area addressed by the seventh commandment. Faithfulness in marriage is central, but again the principle is to be applied far more widely. The initial concern about tassels may well have something to do with modesty of dress.

Sexual conduct is an important part of any legislation, and

a number of the specific laws here (22:13–30) were ahead of their time when it came to protecting young women. The element of protection was balanced by the ultimate sanction in the case of fornication. They bear the hallmark of divine insight regarding fallen human nature. Neither the man, by falsely accusing a girl of immorality, nor the young woman, by falsely accusing a man of rape, could evade punishment for his or her evil. Another important principle underlies the law stating that a man who violates a woman should marry her. Clearly the act itself constitutes a commitment to the woman that can only be properly honoured by following through with marriage.

Sexual conduct and worship were closely linked in some of the 'abominations' of Canaanite religion, so it is not so big a leap as it might seem to move on to consider exclusions from the assembly of the Lord (23:1–7). The handicap referred to in the initial prohibition probably has reference to a local practice and it's thought that illegitimate children (23:2) were also associated with pagan rituals. Ammonites and Moabites (23:3) were blacklisted too. In seeking to get Balaam to curse Israel, they had only managed to secure their own fate. Regarding Edomites and Egyptians (23:7–8), mitigating factors meant that they were treated more leniently.

There aren't just exclusions from the place of worship; there are also grounds for exclusion from the whole camp (23:9–14). Purity, while especially important in the assembly, is to extend to the whole camp. A 'nocturnal emission' would render a man unclean until evening (23:10). Then he could return to the camp, but only after bathing himself in water. The lesson here would seem to be the same as the one Jesus taught when he said, 'What comes out of a person is what defiles him. For from within, out of the heart of man, come evil thoughts, sexual immorality, theft, murder, adultery, coveting, wickedness, deceit, sensuality, envy, slander, pride, foolishness. All these evil things come from within, and they defile a person' (Mark 7:20–23). We are unclean on the inside—that's the point. Like the Pharisees, we might pride ourselves on keeping the outside respectable, in a good state of repair; but the reality is that we will only be whitewashing all manner of uncleanness within (Matt. 23:25–28). A 'call of nature' would also need to be answered outside the camp (23:12–13). This would be another reminder of our uncleanness, as well as ensuring good hygiene (another kind of purity). It may be natural, but then we are, by nature, unclean in God's sight—natural isn't necessarily good—so the lesson is the same.

The eighth commandment: the property principle (23:15–24:7)

Commandment number eight prohibited stealing, but there are some areas of life where that principle applies that could easily be overlooked. Sheltering an escaped servant (23:15–16) is a duty that presumably springs from Israel's own experience of bondage. Knowing what they have been through ought to make them sympathetic to others in a similar plight.

The laws concerning cult prostitutes should come as no surprise (23:17–18), and prohibiting charging a brother interest (23:19–20) dates back to the initial giving of the law (Exod. 22:25). The enforcing reason given there was God's compassion, which would ensure that if the poor were mistreated, the Lord would be ready to act on their behalf. Far better for the Lord's people to be compassionate in the first place (James 2:15–16; 1 John 3:17).

We should expect a God of truth to require the fulfilling of any voluntary vows that might be made (23:21–23). He keeps his promises and expects us to keep ours. Such vows were entirely voluntary, but it was preferable to refrain from making them, rather than to make and then break them. An unfulfilled vow would make keeping property that had been promised to someone else theft. Again, there is a healthy balance between protecting personal property and guarding against a grasping spirit. The laws about vineyards and standing grain (23:24–25) serve to ensure generosity, with a counter-balance that would stop those who benefit from wrongly taking advantage and exploiting the law in their favour.

> We should expect a God of truth to require the fulfilling of any voluntary vows that might be made. He keeps his promises and expects us to keep ours.

With the laws concerning divorce (24:1–4) we have the advantage of the Lord's explanation, which tells us that certificates of divorce were a kind of 'necessary evil' in so far as they were only permitted because of the hardness of heart of the Lord's people (Matt. 19:8). Wives were often mistreated by their husbands, as if they were their 'property'. The idea of certificates was to guard the rights of the wife and to make any 'sending away' something official. It should have made the husband think twice before taking such a serious step. Sadly, we know that the Jewish elders were using this law for a very different purpose in Jesus' day. They viewed it as a kind of get-out clause, adopting a ridiculously broad view of what constituted 'indecency' (Deut. 24:1). While it was supposed to underline the permanence of marriage and limit abuses, it was actually used to cheapen and undermine the institution (not unlike the 'quickie' divorces of the modern day). No doubt the discharge from war and public duty for the first year of marriage (24:5) had the intention of ensuring that good foundations were laid for a relationship that was to last a lifetime.

The law about pledges (24:6) is another mercy law to stop anyone in difficult circumstances from being deprived of his or her means of subsistence.

Being involved directly in the enslaving of an Israelite—someone the Lord had delivered from slavery—was to rob him of his freedom and make you liable to the death penalty (24:7). Stealing people (much like modern-day human trafficking) was the worst kind of breach of the eighth commandment.

The ninth commandment: the justice principle (24:8–25:4)

The connection with the ninth commandment may not be immediately apparent, but Miriam's sin (24:9) was that she 'spoke against' Moses (Num. 12:1). Treating others fairly is the principle at the heart of the ninth commandment, and saying what is right is a big part of that. Much as Lot's wife was to be remembered for the seriousness of her disobedience in turning back to Sodom (Luke 17:32), so Miriam was to be a lasting reminder of the seriousness of libel. The implication was that she and Aaron shared the same status as Moses—a claim that the Lord makes clear was a case of bearing false witness. Leprosy was a disease that needed to be dealt with carefully, according to the Levitical law. The stigma of leprosy emphasized the gravity of the offence, as did the seven-day exclusion from the camp that followed.

Further laws concerning the use of a cloak as a pledge (24:10–13) contain measures to protect the poor, with the assurance that treating the vulnerable well will gain the Lord's approval. The alternative is spelled out in the next law—the cry of the (exploited) poor will reach the Lord's ear and condemnation, rather than commendation, will follow (24:14–15). All too often, the poor are denied justice by authorities ready to believe the false witness of the rich and influential. In Israel, once again, things were to be very different.

Another 'fairness' law enshrines the important principle of personal responsibility and accountability (24:16). While sin has consequences that can stretch across generations in the Lord's providence (Exod. 20:5), when it comes to civil law, there can be no transferring of guilt and punishment.

Other vulnerable folk ('the sojourner … the fatherless … the widow') are to be treated fairly under the law (24:17–18), the motivation to be sympathetic again coming from the memory of Israel's slavery in Egypt. They are also to be treated kindly by Israel's farmers for the same reason (24:19–22).

Another law with the aim of guarding against excess is the one about beating (25:1–3). Forty is the limit. In a creditable show of concern to avoid inadvertently breaking this law it became customary to give only thirty-nine stripes. It was a practice the apostle Paul became all too familiar with (2 Cor. 11:24).

The next law forbidding the muzzling of an ox (25:4) looks like a simple law to ensure that the principle of fairness is extended to animals as well as people. We might have hesitated to see a more general principle at work here, were it not for Paul's application of it in two of his letters. There we learn that it can be applied to Christian workers, who should be supported financially and practically in their spiritual work (1 Cor. 9:9; 1 Tim. 5:18). This inspired application reassures us that we are rightly handling the Scriptures when we see general principles in some of these laws, without giving us licence to allow our imaginations to run riot.

The tenth commandment: the contentment principle (25:5–26:19)

The importance of an inheritance would have been on the minds of the men of Israel just before entering the land, and the perpetuating of the family name was a matter of honour. Thus the marrying of a dead brother's wife (25:5–10) was a family duty which could only be avoided at the cost of bringing shame upon oneself. Why would anybody want to avoid it? Well, there was a cost attached, and that brings us to the tenth commandment. While it prohibits coveting, the antidote to coveting is contentment.

> **The antidote to coveting is contentment.**

'Your neighbour's wife' is the first thing we are warned not to covet in the final commandment, and that is the probable cause of the next problem Moses deals with. Decency seems to be what lies behind the law (and punishment) regarding a woman's hand touching a man at his most vulnerable point (25:11–12). It is perhaps also significant that the parts of the body involved with reproduction are viewed as unclean, possibly indicating the truth that David is acutely aware of in one of his psalms: 'I was brought forth in iniquity, and in sin did my mother conceive me' (Ps. 51:5).

We have already had reason to note that the God of truth abhors dishonesty, not least in the business of buying and selling. The length of enjoyment of the land is—not for the first time—employed as motivation (25:13–16). Weights and measures were at the heart of Israel's trade, and in some ways were the acid test of their honesty.

While the Lord is concerned to ensure that the names of the men of Israel are not blotted out (25:6), the same cannot be said of Amalek (25:17–19). To be blotted out *will* be *their* fate. While Israel are to remember God's gracious dealings with them, they are not to forget the very different treatment they received from the Amalekites.

Chapter 26 is a memory exercise too, and this time the lesson is thankfulness. In Psalm 103 David tells himself to 'Bless the LORD … and forget not all his benefits' (Ps. 103:2). Moses has been reminding the people over and over again, as well as warning them of the dangers of forgetting. The bringing of the firstfruits of the promised land to the Lord (26:1–11) ensures that Israel will regularly remind themselves of all that the Lord has done for them, as well as recalling their humble beginnings. They are to be in no doubt that the very offerings they are bringing were a gift from God to them. Being truly thankful for what we have will help us to 'be content with what [we] have' (Heb. 13:5). Hopefully we can go further: God's goodness should make us generous and joyful (26:11)!

Every harvest would refresh their memories; and if that wasn't enough, every third year was to be a 'year of tithing' to support the Levite and to help 'the sojourner, the fatherless, and the widow' (26:12). Only in following the Lord's commands carefully and completely could they confidently pray for God's blessing on them and their land. The declaration of commitment from the people is more than matched by the Lord's declaration of his commitment to them (26:18–19). It's a promise that Peter tells us is for Christians too (1 Peter 2:9). To be prized now and ultimately promoted to a place of great glory by the Lord our God is a promise and privilege that we should treasure in turn! If that is true of us, shouldn't we be content?

FOR FURTHER STUDY

1. Read Titus 1:15. What do you think Paul means here? What kind of purity is he talking about?
2. Read Matthew 18:21–35. If Israel were to remember their time in slavery, what are we supposed to remember, and how should it affect us?
3. Read 2 Corinthians 1:3–4. How should we make the most of difficult times when we have known God's help?
4. Read Matthew 19:3–9. What is the bill of divorce designed to allow, how had it been abused, and what made it necessary?

TO THINK ABOUT AND DISCUSS

1. Find out the arguments concerning remarriage among those who are committed to the authority of Scripture. What is clear, and what are the grey areas when it comes to actual situations today?
2. What advice would you give to a young couple wanting to lay good foundations for a lifelong relationship?
3. Who are the vulnerable in our day that the church should be showing fairness, compassion and generosity towards? What will that involve?
4. What modern-day forms of deception parallel the false weights and measures of Moses' day?
5. Draw up a list of things to be thankful for, and try to get through a whole week without complaining, enlisting the help of someone close to you who can point out the first hint of a complaint.

Part 3
The rite

9 The covenant

(27:1–30:20)

The plastered stones by the Jordan, the striking hills of Gerizim and Ebal, and the Levites' solemn recital of curses and blessings were the audio-visual equivalents of using bold, italics and underlining together for emphasis. It was all designed to help Israel make the right choice, and then stick to it.

A day to remember (27:1–8)

We have already been warned a number of times in Deuteronomy that God's people tend to have short memories when it comes to the Lord's mercies, but sadly, the same is true when it comes to his law. Moses gives instructions concerning plastered and uncut stones that will serve as two prominent reminders for the people. The copy of the law and the altar are to be a priority. They aren't to be left while Israel address 101 other things that need to be sorted out as they enter the land. This isn't something that they can get round to at some point when things are more settled. It is to be done 'on the day you cross over the Jordan' (27:2).

That there was to be an altar right next to the copy of the law (vv. 5–6) bore eloquent testimony to Israel's inability to keep God's commandments. Their relationship with God could never be maintained on merit—it had to be based on sacrifice. Burnt offerings (v. 6) expressed and represented the devotion to God that Israel owed but failed to give. Peace offerings (v. 7) showed that the breaking of God's law meant a broken relationship that could only be restored through sacrifice.

A day of contrasts (27:9–28:68)

It's a significant day. 'This day' (27:9) is the day when Israel are to formally renew the covenant. To be counted as the Lord's people is its chief privilege, with obedience its chief responsibility. It's a solemn day, too. With six tribes standing on Mount Gerizim, and the other six on Mount Ebal, a list of curses is pronounced. After each individual curse, and then again at the end of the recital, 'all the people' are to voice their agreement. This must have impressed on the people that they weren't just bystanders or spectators at a ceremony: each of them was involved. It couldn't have been clearer: while this covenant was between God and the nation as a whole, it was also a personal covenant made with each individual. Special emphasis is placed on the curses. The audience participation and the geography of the place added to the solemnity of the proceedings, with the two striking hills so close to each other confronting Israel with the two options being set before them:

curse or blessing. There may even have been an echo, leaving the curses and blessings (but especially the curses) ringing in the ears of the people literally as well as metaphorically.

The blessings focused on the farmer's field and the battlefield, and would strike fear into the hearts of their enemies. The curses promised only drought and defeat. As the curses continue and go into more detail we again edge into the area of prophecy, as future captivity is vividly portrayed. As Bob Dylan once sang, 'You gotta serve somebody', and Moses is clear that refusing to serve the Lord will inevitably lead to serving their enemies instead. The apostle Paul is equally clear how stark the choice is. In Romans 6 he makes clear that we are all slaves, either of sin or of obedience (Rom. 6:16–18). The wages on offer for sin's slaves is death, while God's slaves will receive, as an unearned gift, nothing less than eternal life (Rom. 6:21–23). Serving the Lord should be a joyful business, in the light of his goodness and generosity, but we should 'rejoice with trembling' (Ps. 2:11), because this God is also to be feared. If we fail to fear him, we will end up fearing all sorts of other things instead. There is no middle ground here: this Lord is either delighting to show his mercy or delighting to show his justice. We have no grounds for complaint about the latter, but every reason to marvel at the former.

A day to decide (29:1–29)

It's make-your-mind-up time for Israel. They have seen (though without *really* seeing) what the Lord has done for them; the question is what they will now do with his commandments. The choice is clear, but there will always be those who think they can get away with outward conformity, while their heart isn't in it. Moses knows there will be individuals, even clans and tribes (v. 18), like this. They will tell themselves, 'I shall be safe', when nothing could be further from the truth. Israel needed to look out for such characters, and so does the church of Christ (the New Testament letter to the Hebrews quotes Deut. 29:18 from the Septuagint, the Greek translation of the Old Testament, Heb. 12:15). The consequences of allowing such roots to grow and bear fruit will be bitter indeed—and visible. 'Why such devastation?' would be the question on the lips of the surrounding nations; and the answer would come, 'They provoked their God.'

Deuteronomy 29:29 has become a popular proof text. In context it seems to be saying, 'Don't worry so much about what the future holds; concentrate on present obedience.' Take care to keep the covenant and the future will take care of itself. The Lord has a secret will[1] that is being worked out in history and of which we have a very limited grasp, but his revealed will is there for all to see: on the plastered stones and in our Bibles. Jesus had a similar cautionary message for his disciples. They had an unhealthy interest (shared by many Christians since!) in the timing and events surrounding 'the end of the age' (Matt. 24:3–44). Jesus' response was to stress that 'no one knows' (Matt. 24:36) about the timing, and that their primary concern ('But know this …') was to 'be ready' (Matt. 24:43–44). A similar exchange is recorded in the book of Acts, when the disciples ask when Jesus is going to 'restore the kingdom to Israel' (Acts 1:6). 'You don't need to worry about that' is the substance of Jesus' reply; 'your focus is to be on being my witnesses, and for that you're going to need the Holy Spirit' (Acts 1:7–8).

A day to come (30:1–14)

The opening of Deuteronomy 30 has the same message as the old chorus 'There's a way back to God from the dark paths of sin'. Well might Israel be troubled at the detailed depiction of captivity in the previous chapter, but that didn't have to be the end of the story. There was a way back—from disobedience and from Babylon. 'There's a door that is open, and you may go in.' As in the story of the prodigal son, Israel could be sure that they would be welcomed back, provided the return was wholehearted (v. 2). A further promise seems to look forward to the new covenant promised by Jeremiah and Ezekiel (see Jer. 31:31–34; Ezek. 37:24–27). Beyond the return from captivity, the Lord would actually help the people in their hearts to ensure a love for him and his commandments. Obedience would make all the difference.

This commandment, Moses says, is reasonable and achievable (v. 11), and with the commandment the Lord will grant all the help needed to obey it to those who genuinely want to. There's no need to send someone to heaven or across the sea; the word has been delivered right to their door (vv. 12–14). If there is a problem, it won't be with the word; it will be with their own hearts. Paul takes

Moses' words and adapts them to show that it is ultimately Christ who brings, not the law, but righteousness within our reach by descending from heaven and then rising from the dead (Rom. 10:6–11). Having the law in your mouth and heart is one thing; having faith in Christ on your lips and in your heart is quite another. That is what was really meant by a 'circumcised heart'. We don't get one by *doing*, but by *believing*, says Paul.

A day to choose (30:15–20)

We have already seen the stark contrast between blessings and curses. Moses now puts it even more bluntly: 'life and good' or 'death and evil' (v. 15). There are times and seasons that call for decisiveness, and this was one of them. Joshua would challenge the people in days to come to 'choose this day whom you will serve' (Josh. 24:15) and Elijah would ask, centuries later, 'How long will you go limping between two different opinions?' (1 Kings 18:21). Esther had to make a choice before she went to the king (Esth. 4:13–16). In the New Testament, Hebrews makes plain that we too are confronted with a choice every time we hear God's Word (Heb. 3:7–13). In all of these examples the urgency of the situation, the immediacy of the response ('this day', 'How long …?', 'such a time as this', 'Today') and the seriousness of the consequences are clear. Israel had two options: they would either prosper *in* the land or perish *from* the land. It ought to have been an easy choice; but then sinners find it hard to choose what is right, even when it should be obvious.

Choosing life means choosing to love God, and that will involve obeying and 'holding fast to him' (30:20). We have already come across this word five times in Deuteronomy, three times in a similar context (10:20; 11:22; 13:4). The other two occurrences translate the same word as 'stick' and 'cling' respectively (13:17; 28:60). It's the same word used in Genesis 2:24 traditionally translated 'cleave' (KJV). Stickability is what we need: a tendency to be 'drawn away' (30:17) is what we have. The need was the same in Joshua's day (Josh. 22:5; 23:8—where the danger was one of mixing with the nations). Centuries later, King Hezekiah was especially commended for his trust in the Lord (2 Kings 18:5) and the fact that 'he held fast' to him (2 Kings 18:6). What is required is the same resolve shown by Ruth when she said,

> Stickability is what we need: a tendency to be 'drawn away' is what we have.

Do not urge me to leave you or to return from following you. For where you go I will go, and where you lodge I will lodge. Your people shall be my people, and your God my God. Where you die I will die, and there will I be buried. May the LORD do so to me and more also if anything but death parts me from you (Ruth 1:16–17).

It shouldn't be an onerous task—he is, after all, our 'life and length of days' (Deut. 30:20). Simon Peter had it right when the Lord gave him the option of leaving him: 'Lord, to whom shall we go? You have the words of eternal life' (John 6:68). He still has.

For further study ▶

FOR FURTHER STUDY

1. Read Romans 12:1–3 and Hebrews 13:15–16. What sorts of offerings should Christians bring to God?
2. Read Romans 6:12–19. When Paul speaks of 'presenting' and 'not presenting' in this passage, what will that look like in practice?
3. Read Hebrews 12:15. What are the similarities between the situation Hebrews is addressing and that which Moses was dealing with?
4. Read Romans 10:5–8. Is Paul saying that this is the real meaning of the passage in Deuteronomy, or is he just using it and adapting it for illustrative purposes?

TO THINK ABOUT AND DISCUSS

1. Do you know the Ten Commandments off by heart? If not, learn them!
2. What do you think of the old practice of making a formal covenant with God? What are the pros and cons? How about whole churches entering into church covenants?
3. When was the last time you had a choice to make and it was a struggle to choose what was right?
4. How might the difference between God's secret will and his revealed will help us in the area of guidance?

10 The successor

(31:1–29)

Both the people and their new leader, Joshua, will need to be strong, courageous and obedient going forward. They are given two things to help: the assurance of God's presence and a written copy of the law—a reminder of their covenant privileges and a record of their covenant obligations.

The book of Deuteronomy is a book of transition in many ways, and this chapter signals the imminent changing of the guard. The nation as a whole, Joshua, the priests, Moses and the Levites are all given their marching orders as the time to strike camp draws near.

Charge to all Israel, Joshua and the priests (31:1–13)

Moses begins with a bad news/good news combination. The bad news is that Moses will not be leading them into the promised land. The good news is that the Lord their God will! The Lord will do to their enemies what he has promised; they must do what they have been commanded. Fear and dread should have no place in their hearts with the Lord at their head (v. 6). Strength and courage are the order of the day. In fact, there won't be too many days when strength and courage won't be needed. We need them too. Happily, though, there won't be *any* days for the people of Israel to face on their own—their God will not forsake them. They have seen what happened to Sihon and Og (v. 4); Adoni-zedek, Jabin and their confederates will go the same way. Believing God's promises is where the needed strength and courage come from. Here the promise is that 'the Lord will give them over to you, and you shall do to them according to the whole commandment that I have commanded you' (v. 5).

Next, Moses promises Joshua, 'you shall go with this people ... and you shall put them in possession of it' (v. 7). It's a promise that the Lord repeats to Joshua directly, after Moses' death (Josh. 1:6). After his victory over the Amorite kings, Joshua similarly encourages his chiefs: 'For thus the Lord will do to all your enemies' (Josh. 10:25). Solomon has a promise to encourage him as well—'He shall build a house' (1 Chr. 22:10, 13)—along with a promise that the work will be finished (1 Chr. 28:20). Hezekiah, too, assures the people, 'there are more with us than with [the king of Assyria]' (2 Chr. 32:7). Every one of these promises is given with one purpose: that the people concerned might 'be strong and courageous'.

Moses' charge to Joshua is the same as that to the people (v. 7). Joshua will need exactly the same qualities that his people need. He is to lead by example. The promise to all Israel of the Lord's presence and help is a promise to each individual, too, with the added reassurance that this is no temporary arrangement. Who can doubt that Joshua was all the stronger for having both the exhortation and the promise addressed to him personally? It's what we're supposed to do with God's promises—appropriate them for ourselves. Joshua would be reminded of them at various points as time went on, just as our memories need jogging from time to time (not least by the bread and wine of the Lord's Supper—Luke 22:19; 1 Cor. 11:24–25).

If we're honest, God doesn't always *seem* to be with us—so we need reassuring, and we need faith to believe the reassurance. He really has promised never to leave or forsake his people. David would take this ancient promise and apply it to his son Solomon (1 Chr. 28:20). It was just as encouraging when it came to building temples as it was for fighting battles. And then, centuries later, the writer of Hebrews applies it to Christians of the first century facing poverty and persecution (Heb. 13:5). The Greek could hardly be more emphatic,[1] and the writer makes it clear that these words came to Joshua directly from God. He makes two points: these Christians aren't facing their trials alone, and they can face them content with what they have. 'The LORD is my shepherd; I shall not want' (Ps. 23:1) is the conclusion they are being invited to draw. We can preach the same promises with the same confidence today.

> If we're honest, God doesn't always *seem* to be with us—so we need reassuring, and we need faith to believe the reassurance.

The priests had an important task to perform every seven years (vv. 9–13). That was how often 'all Israel' (in the broadest sense—'men, women, and little ones, and the sojourner') were to be solemnly reminded of the law. They needed to both 'hear and learn to fear the LORD' (v. 13). Proof of the latter would be seen in their carefully doing 'all the words of this law' (v. 12).

Charge to Moses (31:14–29)

Moses and Joshua present themselves before the Lord for a formal commissioning of the new leader, but first Moses is given a glimpse of the future. The covenant will be broken, and the idolatry of the people will mean that the Lord will forsake them. The promise of his presence hangs on the obedience of the people. If they forsake him (v. 16), they will find that he will forsake them (v. 17). That will spell disaster. And this isn't just a warning: some earlier passages have had a prophetic element to them and here it is much clearer. The Lord is emphatically declaring what will happen. Israel's wickedness will be great, and their troubles many. And the Lord knows what will happen next—they'll blame him (v. 17)! They will question his faithfulness and love, and accuse him of deserting them. We all have this tendency to question, and, by implication, to accuse God when things are difficult. Sometimes we will say only that we don't understand, but often what we are really thinking and feeling is, 'It's not fair!' Ever since Adam rather deftly passed the buck to Eve and managed to subtly point out that she had been a gift from God, we have been 'inclined' (v. 21) to follow 'It's not fair!' with 'It's not my fault', closely followed by 'And actually, thinking about it, the Lord is ultimately to blame'. Of course, it is the language of our hearts—we rarely dare to put into words what we are really thinking and feeling; but the Lord looks on the heart and hears what it is saying as clear as a bell.

Excuses are a fact of life. Whether it is an explanation for the absence of homework or for being late, it is amazing how creative we can be. We're all able fig-leaf manufacturers when it comes to covering up our sins. Almost anything other than a frank admission of guilt seems to be preferable. Amusing examples of (allegedly) real accident reports submitted with car insurance claims can be found on the Internet, such as:

'I started to slow down but the traffic was more stationary than I thought.'

'I didn't think the speed limit applied after midnight.'

'I collided with a stationary truck coming the other way.'

'I had been shopping for plants all day and was on my way home. As I reached an intersection, a hedge sprang up, obscuring my vision, and I did not see the other car.'

'The accident happened because I had one eye on the lorry in front, one eye on the pedestrian, and the other on the car behind.'

'As I approached an intersection, a sign suddenly appeared in a place where no stop sign had ever appeared before.'

'No one was to blame for the accident, but it would never have happened if the other driver had been alert.'[2]

They are amusing, but our own inventive attempts to dodge responsibility for our actions might well be laughable too. Many excuses that people come up with are improbable, while others are very plausible; but it is amazing to see the lengths to which we will go to avoid blame. And if we can't think of an excuse, we can easily become blame-shifters, looking for a scapegoat to carry the can.

The better reaction to difficulties in our lives is modelled for us in various parts of Scripture, but we will need to come to terms with our sinfulness first. Only then will we be ready to echo Ezra's confession: 'And after all that has come upon us for our evil deeds and for our great guilt, seeing that you, our God, have punished us less than our iniquities deserved ...' (Ezra 9:13). Considering what Israel had gone through, that was quite an admission. We usually feel the pain of the punishment far more than we feel the seriousness of the sin. David is another good example of the opposite—though it is sad to recognize the depths to which he had to go to learn the lesson. In Psalm 51 we see him excusing God rather than himself when he confesses his sin, saying, 'Against you ... have I sinned ... so that you may be justified in your words and blameless in your judgement' (Ps. 51:4). He goes on to acknowledge his sinfulness, as well as his particular sins, and recognizes that he has a heart problem that only God can put right. He also knows that he is guilty of bloodshed (51:14), for which there was no sacrifice, so he is entirely dependent on God's mercy. David shows us that, instead of condemning God and justifying ourselves, the gracious response in the midst of difficulty is to do precisely the opposite. Later, as some of the consequences of his sin begin to play out, we see just how humbled by his sin David has been. He knows that he has no grounds for complaint when his beloved and over-loved (in the sense of spoiled) son Absalom rebels. David meekly accepts the Lord's discipline as he leaves Jerusalem, saying, 'If I find favour in the eyes of the LORD, he will bring me back and let me see both it and his dwelling place. But if he says, "I have no pleasure in you", behold, here I am, let him do to me what seems good to him' (2 Sam. 15:26). That's how to be 'trained' by the Lord's discipline (Heb. 12:11).

Israel and another nation I like to call 'Weaswell' (We–as–well) are 'rebellious and stubborn' (Deut. 31:27). We get things terribly wrong and then fail to recognize or accept what a mess we've made. So what might bring us to our senses? Well, a written record of the Lord's warnings and prophecies could help us. And even if we fail to benefit from it, there will at least be evidence to clear the Lord of any charges of unfairness or unfaithfulness. When we have our doubts about somebody's ability or determination to follow through on a promise we sometimes ask, 'Can I have that in writing?' The idea is to get some written evidence to remind that person of his or her words when it's more convenient for him or her to forget them. There is no escaping the Lord's words either.

It's always worth thinking ahead about what might happen in the future and thinking about safeguards that we can put in place that will help to keep us on the straight and narrow. The frightening thing is that backsliders are not very good at recognizing that they're backsliding. We need all the help we can get. We won't all have a Nathan, as David did, to confront us when we are in denial about our sins (2 Sam. 12:1–14). But we will have the Scriptures, and they'll be straight with us concerning wrongdoing. That's why John Bunyan wrote in the cover of his Bible, 'This book will keep you from sin, or sin will keep you from this book.'[3]

So even if we do go astray in the future, the Bible will be there to help us cut through a lot of muddy thinking and get us back on track. It stands as a witness to the unblemished character of God and the rather different story about our own wandering hearts.

But even in our darkest days we can turn to the Scriptures—and to the Song of Moses …

FOR FURTHER STUDY

1. Read 2 Timothy 2:1–13. What truths does Paul encourage Timothy to draw strength from here?
2. Read 2 Samuel 12. What tactics did Nathan use to bring David to his senses, and why?
3. Read Psalm 51:1–14. In how many ways does David stress the seriousness of his sin?
4. Read Daniel 9:3–19. What sins does Daniel confess, and what is the basis of his pleas to God?
5. Read Psalm 119:1–32 (or the whole psalm!). According to these verses, what do we need to do with God's Word in order to derive maximum benefit from it?

TO THINK ABOUT AND DISCUSS

1. What would you say to someone who is of the opinion that a Bible promise doesn't apply to him or her?
2. What are the most common ways in which we shift the blame off ourselves and onto something or someone else?
3. What has made you question or even accuse God? How did you eventually deal with it?
4. What might bring us to our senses in a period of backsliding?
5. Can you think of any safeguards you could put in place to keep you on track?
6. Which Bible verses would you least like to be confronted with at the moment, and why?

11 The song

(31:30–32:52)

In many ways, the book of Deuteronomy is a book of stark contrasts, and this song is no different. It celebrates the greatness, wisdom, justice, faithfulness and uprightness of God. It also mourns the weakness, folly, corruption, forgetfulness and crookedness of his people. It's a song for all times, and a song for us.

At the end of chapter 31 Moses expresses his intention to address the people and to 'call heaven and earth to witness against them' (31:28). That's where his song begins. Moses expresses his desire to be heard—really heard (32:1). It's one thing to speak 'in the ears' of someone, but quite another for the words to 'sink into' someone's ears (as Jesus put it, Luke 9:44). But even if the assembly of Israel doesn't listen to his words, heaven and earth will. Not only does Moses want his words to be heard, he also has a desire to bless the people. His words have the potential to refresh and revive. After all, the main theme of his song is a refreshing one: 'the name of the LORD'. The secondary theme is less so: the character of the people.

A just and upright God and a crooked and twisted generation (32:1–5)

Moses is going to 'proclaim the name of the LORD' (v. 3). We can look back to Exodus 34:5 where the Lord himself did the same thing. So why is it that the Lord said something rather different there from what Moses says here? To 'proclaim the name of the LORD' is another way of saying to 'declare what God is like'. His 'name' is his character. There is a big overlap between the two passages, but a different emphasis too.

God is great: great in his works and great in his ways. The greatness of his power was on display at the Red Sea and celebrated in Moses' first song (Exod. 15:7, 16). The greatness of his steadfast love had also been shown as he repeatedly forgave Israel throughout their wilderness wanderings (Num. 14:19). They, like the tribe of Reuben (Gen. 49:4), have been 'unstable as water'; he has been as solid as a rock (Deut. 32:4). This is the first time in Scripture that God is described as 'the Rock'. In no time at all Moses uses the same term five times (vv. 4, 15, 18, 30–31); reliability is what he is trying to get across. God's work (v. 4), his salvation (v. 15), his fatherly care (v. 18), his discipline (v. 30) and his presence (v. 31) can all be relied upon.

David looked back to this song when he composed one of his own. It is a variation on a theme, and again—five times—he refers to God as his rock (2 Sam. 22:2–3, 32, 47; 23:3). David is thinking of God as a rock primarily in terms of a place of refuge, probably remembering his days on the run from Saul (see 1 Sam. 23:25; 1 Chr. 11:15). It's a theme he returns to in his psalms time and time again (Ps. 18:2, 31, 46; 19:14; 28:1; 31:2–3; 61:2; 62:2, 6–7; 144:1). It's a timeless truth that Isaiah, Habakkuk and every Christian can keep returning to as well, because he is 'an *everlasting* rock' (Isa. 26:4; Hab. 1:12, emphasis added).

Nothing has been lacking in all that God has done for his people—his work has been, and always is, 'perfect' (Deut. 32:4). Nobody could accuse him of injustice. He has been more than fair at every point of their journey—in a word, *faithful*. Here is another term applied to God for the first time here in Deuteronomy and which proves to be a theme for Israel's praise over the centuries (see Ps. 33:4; 36:5; 40:10; 89:1–2, 5, 8, 24, 33, 49; 92:2; 96:13; 98:3; 100:5; 119:75, 90; 143:1), where it is often coupled with the Hebrew word translated (in the ESV) 'steadfast love'.[1] 'Rock' is the picture, but '*faithfulness*' is the quality. The word appears once in Exodus, where it is translated 'steady' (Exod. 17:12). Something that is faithful can be leaned on, depended on. Someone who is faithful deserves our faith (or trust). Israel, though, are a group of 'children in whom is no faithfulness' (Deut. 32:20). They have been a handful every step of the way. While God's dealings with them have been beyond reproach, they 'have dealt corruptly with him' (v. 5). Where he has been 'without iniquity' (v. 4), they 'are blemished' (v. 5). The final contrast is even more striking—'just and upright' is rather different from 'crooked and twisted'.

A senseless people and a caring God (32:6–14)

Next, Israel are accused of being 'senseless' in their response to their Lord (v. 6). They had failed to take on board the special treatment they had received over the centuries. A quick look back over their history would tell them that Israel owed its very existence to this God. He had chosen the nation (v. 9), created it and established it (v. 6), and cared for it (vv. 10–11). He had guided it (v. 12) and provided for it (vv. 13–14). The care had been tender and thorough. The provision had been miraculous, generous and of top quality. Yet all this had been lost on Israel. 'Senseless'—or as we would put it today, 'stupid'—is about right! Our own personal history tells much the same story, though. Less of the miraculous, but many of the same blessings, and many of the same sins.

A provoking people and a provoking God (32:15–25)

The saddest thing of all was that it was the blessings that led to the sins. They overindulged when the blessings came, and turned away from God as they did so (v. 15). The name 'Jeshurun' is an unusual one and is used of Israel only three other times: twice in the next chapter (33:5, 26) and once in Isaiah (Isa. 44:2). It comes from a Hebrew word meaning 'upright', and is probably used with some irony here to remind them of what they were supposed to be, though it appears to be used affectionately and encouragingly on the other occasions when it is employed.

As they turned away from 'the Rock', they turned towards

'strange gods' (v. 16) that weren't really gods at all. No longer dependent on God, they were no longer mindful of him. It was conduct calculated to provoke a jealous God to anger. And to action! The punishment would fit the crime. They would be provoked to jealousy and anger in their turn, by a foreign nation. Disaster, drought, disease and distress would all be experienced by a 'perverse' people (v. 20). Even death is alluded to with the mention of 'Sheol' (v. 22).[2] There would be no hiding place from the disasters that would come (v. 25); male and female, young and old will have to face the consequences of their abominations.

A foolish people and a compassionate God (32:26–38)

If forgetting God is one way of provoking him, there is another: robbing him of his glory. That happens when his chosen instrument of discipline takes credit for the judgement without acknowledging the Lord's role or purpose in it—especially when that instrument is so bold as to deny it.

Israel should have been capable of working it out for themselves. They were supposed to ask, 'How did we get into such a mess?' and they ought to have come up with the correct answer: 'The Lord has left us to our own devices as a punishment for our disobedience.' It is a sad state of affairs when the enemies of God's people are in the ascendancy, but even when that is the case it is still true that they are 'by themselves' (v. 31). They have no 'Rock' to help them. Their 'gods' have only small 'g's—and that means that their superiority will not last. The Lord has his plans for them, ready and waiting. When the time comes those plans will be carried out with speed. Both vengeance and vindication are in the Lord's hands, and we are supposed to leave them there (see Rom. 12:19; Heb. 10:30). When wronged, we can daydream about the exposing and downfall of those who have mistreated us. We can fantasize about the day when we will be vindicated before a watching world. But if we don't nip such thoughts in the bud, we may even begin to take matters into our own hands, as we attempt to turn our imaginings into reality. 'Don't!' says the Word of God. 'Leave it with the Lord and leave it to the Lord' (see Rom. 12:19). He will deal with it. He has a 'time' and a 'day' set to sort things out. Why? Because the Lord will 'have compassion on his servants' (v. 36). When he sees them struggling and weak, he cares, and prepares a rescue plan. Similarly, when he sees the vicious and the proud on the rise, he is already anticipating their downfall. They can't be allowed to conclude that their gods have given them the victory. Instead, the day will come when their gods are shown up for the helpless, powerless nothings they really are.

The only God (32:39–43)

When false gods are exposed as fakes, the true God is seen in his sovereign glory. Israel is to have no gods before him because there is no god beside him. What's more, there is no avoiding him and no stopping him—which makes hating him (v. 41) or his children (v. 43) a very bad move. This God will prevail. Whether it is over other 'gods' or his people's enemies, he will ultimately win out, and his people will be 'more than conquerors' (Rom. 8:37).

> When false gods are exposed as fakes, the true God is seen in his sovereign glory.

The only way (32:44–47)

This is a song that needs to be taken to heart (v. 46), along with the rest of Moses' words. They were to be taught, *and* applied, to the next generation. We are used to speeches designed to grab headlines or elicit applause but which prove to be empty and ineffective. The Lord's words are very different. They are full: full of warning; full of promise; and full of potential for those who have ears to hear. They never return to the Lord 'empty', but accomplish his purposes (Isa. 55:11). Their truth could be life-enhancing and—as far as Israel's time in the land is concerned—life-lengthening.

Moses' sight of the land (32:48–52)

Because Moses saw red at the waters of Meribah, he only gets to *see* the land of Canaan. Admittedly, he was provoked by the quarrelling of the people, but that did not excuse him. Here the Lord sums up where he went wrong in two ways. Looking at the original account we find that Moses failed to follow orders. He had been told to speak to the rock, but instead he struck it twice (probably indicating an element of temper, Num. 20:8, 11). He also claimed the credit for producing the water ('shall we … ?', 20:10). Here in Deuteronomy we are told that this disobedience amounted to 'breaking faith' with the Lord (32:51) and a failure to 'treat [the Lord] as holy' in front of the people. Thus Moses added irreverence to his disobedience. If a slip like that on Moses' part led to such consequences, the importance of Israel's keeping faith and fearing the Lord was clear.

FOR FURTHER STUDY

1. Read Hebrews 2:1–4; 3:7–12. What advice do we get in these passages about how to hear God's Word, and what motivations do they supply?

2. Read Matthew 17:17; Luke 9:41; Acts 2:40; and Philippians 2:15. What particular problems with the generation are highlighted by these verses in their contexts?

3. Read Psalm 37. What truths does the psalmist mention that can help us not to fret but to leave those who wrong us with the Lord?

4. Read Isaiah 41:1–4; 43:10–15; 44:6–8; 48:12–14. What is unique about Israel's God, according to these passages?

5. Which Bible incidents can you think of where false gods were shown to be just that: false?

6. Can you think of incidents in the Bible when apparently minor slips received apparently harsh punishment? What was the explanation? Is there a lesson in these incidents?

TO THINK ABOUT AND DISCUSS

1. What is particularly wrong with our generation?

2. How many different names of God, and of Jesus in particular, can you think of? What are your favourites, and why?

3. Can you think of times in your own life when blessings led to sins? What went wrong?

4. When was the last time you lost your temper? Why? What can you learn from it?

5. What does 'treating the Lord as holy' look like in everyday life?

12 The blessing

(33:1–34:12)

The book of Deuteronomy closes with a song (or poem) of victory. The song begins with a procession following a coronation, and closes with a declaration of victory. The themes of coming, crowning and conquering ensure that we finish Deuteronomy thinking about an even greater prophet than Moses.

When the Lord came (33:1–5)

Moses' final blessing begins with a poetic description of a coronation at Mount Sinai, then of a procession through the wilderness. The Lord had been formally recognized as Israel's king at Sinai, where the people accepted his law. After that they travelled, via Seir, to Mount Paran, and the Lord had been with them every step of the way. Seir was the region of the wilderness wanderings (see 2:1), and Paran, the place from which the spies were despatched (Num. 13:3) and where the people subsequently refused to enter the land (Num. 13:26). Now, after receiving the law for a second time, they have a second chance. This time they can enter in. God has led them[1] in love to the threshold of the promised land. Moses' message is that the Lord is still their king and remains at the head of the people as they stand poised to conquer Canaan. The procession has not yet reached its destination, but it will. The Lord's intention is to bless his people. Just how he will do that is the subject of the following verses, with their specific promises to the individual tribes. Although it is a *promised* land, its inhabitants will be no pushover. Soon they will be at war, but with the Lord leading them, and the blessings that follow[2] sustaining them, they can go forward with confidence.

Every Christian is at war with foes even more formidable than Canaanites (the world, the flesh and the devil), but the same Lord gives familiar assurances of his blessing to those engaged in the fight of faith.

Reuben (33:6)

As Reuben was Jacob's firstborn, this tribe has the pre-eminence when it comes to the order of blessing (just like the original blessing of Reuben back in Genesis, Gen. 49:3). Reuben's sin with Bilhah (Gen. 35:22), however, meant that he would not be the most blessed. His tribe would survive, but that would be about it. The number of descendants was seen as a reflection of God's favour, and the tribe of Reuben would remain small.[3]

Judah (33:7)

Judah's pre-eminence lay in their position at the head of

Israel's army (Num. 2:9). Well might they pray for a safe return from battle! Here they are encouraged with a prayer/blessing assuring them that their prayers will be heard and their warriors helped.

Levi (33:8–11)

The tribe of Levi had the responsibility, in the person of the high priest, of determining the Lord's will in important matters, and Moses asks the Lord to guide them accordingly. The giving of Thummim and Urim was a promise of guidance from the Lord, enabling the tribe, in turn, to guide the people. There is no detailed explanation of how God's will was revealed by these objects, but their function is clear enough.

The story is told of a young curate in the Church of England who was helped in his understanding of the Bible through conversations with an uneducated cobbler familiar with the Scriptures. On one occasion, he mentioned the cobbler to a visiting friend who was a budding theologian. Confident that he could bamboozle the cobbler with a single question, the theologian asked the cobbler for an explanation of the Urim and Thummim. The cobbler replied that he didn't know exactly, but that through them the high priest was able to find out the Lord's will. 'But,' he went on, picking up his Bible, 'I find that I can get the mind of the Lord by just changing a couple of letters. I take this blessed book, and by usin' and thummin' it I get the mind of the Lord that way!'

As long as Israel sought God's guidance, God, through his appointed means, would give it (see 1 Sam. 14:41–42; Ezra 2:63).

This tribe, in the persons of Moses and Aaron, had got

things wrong under pressure at Massah/Meribah (v. 8). In the original accounts (Exod. 17:1–7; Num. 20:1–13) we are told that the people had tested the Lord (Exod. 17:2, 7). Here Moses points out that, viewed from a different angle, it had been a test for him and Aaron too—sadly one that they failed.[4]

Happily, that wasn't the whole story. At a critical moment in Israel's history the tribe of Levi had risen to the occasion. They had the distinction of having remained faithful to the covenant when all the other tribes had turned to their handmade golden calf (Exod. 32:26–29). Their obedience had been unique, but also costly. The solemn task of executing justice fell to them, and their own families had not been exempt. Would they stand alone against the idolatry of the people? Yes. Would they be prepared to administer justice, even when their loved ones were to be executed? Yes. They weren't being heartless any more than Jesus was encouraging an unfeeling attitude to family when he talked about 'hating' father, mother or brother (Matt. 10:37; Luke 14:26); it was meant only in a comparative sense. Simply put, God must come first—a clear first.

The Levites had set Israel an example. Their main responsibilities focused on teaching and offering. They represented God to the people as they taught his truth, and represented the people before the Lord as they offered sacrifices (v. 10). In both of these key areas they are assured of the Lord's blessing. As the teachers of the nation Levi were dependent on the other tribes to provide for them, so a prayer that the Lord would bless the tribe's substance was apt (v. 11). The request that God would 'accept the work of his hands' is designed to reassure the priests that the offerings they make on behalf of themselves and the people will not be offered in vain. Any opposition they might face (and faithfulness often leads to opposition) would be fully and finally 'crushed' by the Lord.

Benjamin (33:12)

The tribe of Benjamin is beloved and protected, and the Lord is with them. It sounds so very simple, but for a tribe that would become known as 'the least of the tribes of Israel' it must have been a wonderful blessing to hold on to. Christians who feel themselves to be 'the least of all the saints' (Eph. 3:8) can find comfort in the same truths (e.g. 1 Cor. 15:58).

Benjamin will not only have the comfort of dwelling in safety themselves, but will also enjoy the privilege of providing the location for the Lord's dwelling place. Jerusalem lay within Benjamin's territory, and the word 'shoulders' is used to describe a ridge nearby (see Josh. 15:8; 18:16).[5]

Joseph (33:13–17)

Fruitfulness is the key blessing for the two tribes of Joseph. Both *quality* (the same Hebrew word, translated 'choicest', 'finest', 'abundance' and 'best gifts', is used five times in vv. 13–16) and *quantity* are to be enjoyed by Ephraim and Manasseh. Joseph had chosen the name 'Ephraim' for his second son because it sounds like the Hebrew for 'making fruitful'. The Lord had made him fruitful in the land of his affliction (Gen. 41:52), but now comes the promise that both tribes will continue to be fruitful in the land of milk and honey the Lord is giving them. These blessings are only one manifestation of the favour of God that they will enjoy. It will also extend to warfare, where they will be a force to be reckoned with, achieving future expansion.

Zebulun, Issachar and Gad (33:18–21)

For Zebulun and Issachar, an idyllic picture of everyday life[6] is painted, one which is characterized by peace and security, combined with plentiful resources and profitable commerce. Their land will be placed where they can profit from sea trade and naturally occurring products such as dye from shellfish and glass made from sand. Gad had asked for land east of the Jordan because it was so suitable for livestock—what could rightly be described as 'the best of the land' (v. 21). To their credit, they would keep their promise to fight with Israel as they took the land beyond the Jordan. Thus they deserved 'a commander's portion' and faithfully 'executed the justice of the LORD' on the Canaanites.

Dan, Naphtali and Asher (33:22–25)[7]

The reference to 'a lion's cub' suggests that Dan is a tribe with youthful vigour and potential for the future. Naphtali, too, will enjoy the now familiar combination of favour and blessing. Their stretch of land will be both beautiful and fertile. When the Lord blesses, he does so to the point of satisfaction—'to the full'. There is a special blessing for Asher (whose name means 'blessed')—becoming 'the favourite of his brothers'. Their allotted land will prove to be an olive-growing region producing oil in abundance. Over the years they will bear the brunt of many an invasion, but they will survive them all. In short, they will enjoy plenty, protection and power for all they will face, as long as they need it.

While we have specific blessings for the tribes here, there are recurring themes that cover the whole of Israel and apply equally to us in the twenty-first century. The promises have in many ways been reiterated in the New Testament and in some ways intensified. There is a change in emphasis, though. Material blessings rightly take second place to spiritual blessings in the gospel age. While we are still to acknowledge all good gifts as coming from God, the fully formed Christian hope shifts our focus from the present to the future.

> While we are still to acknowledge all good gifts as coming from God, the fully formed Christian hope shifts our focus from the present to the future.

The Lord appeared at the beginning of Moses' blessing as the unique lawgiver and lover of his people. At the close he appears again, the same unique God, this time coming to the rescue of his people (Ps. 18:10). He comes to be with them as a place of refuge, and he comes to uphold them, acting as a kind of safety net (vv. 26–27). He is with them, under them, and—when it comes to battle—goes before them. Safety and plenty were from him. Saved, safeguarded and strengthened against their enemies, Israel were a unique people with a unique God.

It seems fitting that a book about new beginnings should end with a sense of déjà vu. Centuries before, the Lord had told

Abram to lift up his eyes and look (Gen. 13:14). Everything he saw would be given to him and his descendants. This was more than a promise—something more approaching a transaction. And so it is with Moses. Being shown the land (34:1–4) is, in itself, effectively a transfer of ownership. So there is a kind of closure at the end of the book. And yet Moab is not the finish line. The writer is at pains to point out that Moses' failure to enter the promised land wasn't because of old age and ill-health. No, it was 'according to the word of the LORD' (34:5). Not only were the God of Israel and the nation of Israel unique; so was Moses. Despite his intimacy with God, the signs and wonders, and the great deeds, the story wasn't to end with Moses.

The final paragraph acts as a 'To be continued' caption at the end of the book: continued in the safe hands of Joshua. Moses had led the people out of Egypt, and Joshua would lead them into Canaan. And one day, another Joshua[8] would come, able to lead *his* people into blessings that the promised land could only dimly foreshadow.

For further study ▶

FOR FURTHER STUDY

1. Where in the New Testament can we find parallel promises of God's love, God's protection and our safety?
2. What evidence would you point to that shows that Jesus' sacrifice has been accepted?
3. Read Psalm 18:7–16 and Habakkuk 3:3–15. What are the similarities and differences between these passages and the opening of Moses' song?

TO THINK ABOUT AND DISCUSS

1. What blessings are Christians promised when it comes to their spiritual battles?
2. What kind of fruitfulness can we expect as Christians, and what can we do to promote it?
3. Are there any ways in which the Lord guides us other than the Bible? How can we guard against being mistaken?

Appendix

Deuteronomy quotes in the New Testament in New Testament order:	
Matt. 4:4	Deut. 8:3
Matt. 4:7	Deut. 6:16
Matt. 4:10	Deut. 6:13
Matt. 5:21	Deut. 5:17
Matt. 5:27	Deut. 5:18
Matt. 5:31	Deut. 24:1
Matt. 5:38	Deut. 19:21
Matt. 15:4	Deut. 5:16
Matt. 18:16	Deut. 19:15
Matt. 19:7	Deut. 24:1
Matt. 19:18–19	Deut. 5:16–20
Matt. 22:24	Deut. 25:5
Matt. 22:37	Deut. 6:5
Mark 7:10	Deut. 5:16
Mark 10:4	Deut. 24:1
Mark 10:19	Deut. 5:16–20
Mark 12:19	Deut. 25:5
Mark 12:29–33	Deut. 6:4–5
Luke 4:4	Deut. 8:3
Luke 4:8	Deut. 6:13
Luke 4:12	Deut. 6:16
Luke 10:27	Deut. 6:5
Luke 18:20	Deut. 5:16–20
Luke 20:28	Deut. 25:5

Deuteronomy quotes in the New Testament in Deuteronomy order:	
Deut. 4:24	Heb. 12:29
Deut. 4:35	Mark 12:32
Deut. 5:16–21	Matt. 5:21; 15:4; 19:18–19; Mark 7:10; 10:19; Luke 18:20; Rom. 7:7; 13:9; Eph. 6:2–3; James 2:11
Deut. 6:4–5	Matt. 22:37; Mark 12:29–33; Luke 10:27
Deut. 6:13	Matt. 4:10; Luke 4:8
Deut. 6:16	Matt. 4:7; Luke 4:12
Deut. 8:3	Matt. 4:4; Luke 4:4
Deut. 9:4	Rom. 10:6
Deut. 9:19	Heb. 12:21
Deut. 17:6	Heb. 10:28
Deut. 17:7	1 Cor. 5:13
Deut. 18:15–19	Acts 3:12, 22–23; 7:37
Deut. 19:15	Matt. 18:16; 2 Cor. 13:1
Deut. 19:21	Matt. 5:38
Deut. 21:23	Gal. 3:13
Deut. 24:1–3	Matt. 5:31; 19:7; Mark 10:4

Acts 3:22–23	Deut. 18:15–19
Acts 7:37	Deut. 18:15
Rom. 7:7	Deut. 5:21
Rom. 10:6–8	Deut. 9:4; 30:12–14
Rom. 10:19	Deut. 32:21
Rom. 11:8	Deut. 29:4
Rom. 12:19	Deut. 32:35
Rom. 13:9	Deut. 5:17–19, 21
Rom. 15:10	Deut. 32:43
1 Cor. 5:13	Deut. 17:7
1 Cor. 9:9	Deut. 25:4
2 Cor. 13:1	Deut. 19:15
Gal. 3:10	Deut. 27:26
Gal. 3:13	Deut. 21:23
Eph. 6:2–3	Deut. 5:16
1 Tim. 5:18	Deut. 25:4
Heb. 1:6	Deut. 32:43
Heb. 10:28	Deut. 17:6; 19:15
Heb. 10:30	Deut. 32:35–36
Heb. 12:29	Deut. 4:24
James 2:11	Deut. 5:17–18

Deut. 24:14	Mark 10:19
Deut. 25:4–5	Matt. 22:24; Mark 12:19; Luke 20:28; 1 Cor. 9:9; 1 Tim. 5:18
Deut. 27:26	Gal. 3:10
Deut. 29:3–4	Rom. 11:8
Deut. 30:12–14	Rom. 10:6–8
Deut. 31:6–8	Heb. 13:5
Deut. 32:21	Rom. 10:19
Deut. 32:35–36	Rom. 12:19; Heb. 10:30
Deut. 32:43	Rom. 15:10; Heb. 1:6

Endnotes

Background and summary

1 Samuel is perhaps the likeliest candidate.
2 Hittite treaties in particular have been discovered with a remarkably similar structure to the book of Deuteronomy.
3 While some of the laws in Deuteronomy don't seem to fit naturally under the heading of each commandment—leading to some debate among commentators as to whether this outline is real or imagined—the basic structure, despite the odd puzzling inclusion, seems to be unmistakeable.
4 4:8, 26, 38–40; 5:1, 3; 6:6; 7:11; 8:1, 11, 18–19; 9:1, 3; 10:13; 11:2, 4?, 8, 13, 26–28, 32; 12:8?; 13:18; 15:5, 15; 19:9; 26:16–18; 27:1, 4, 9–10; 28:1, 13–15; 29:10–11, 14–15, 18; 30:2, 8, 11, 15–16, 18–19; 32:46.

Chapter 1

1 As opposed to their refusal to go into the land at Kadesh-barnea (Num. 14:1–10).
2 Elsewhere in the Bible it is usually called Sinai, but in Deuteronomy the name Horeb is used.
3 Aristotle, *Nicomachean Ethics*, Book II, Para 8, cited at The Internet Classics Archive, classics.mit.edu.

Chapter 3

1 Edward E. Ericson, Jr., 'Solzhenitsyn: Voice from the Gulag', *Eternity* (October 1985), pp. 23–24; cited at 'Aleksandr Solzhenitsyn', Wikipedia, https://en.wikipedia.org; accessed July 2015.
2 'Horeb' seems to be used interchangeably with 'Sinai', though the former may sometimes be used to describe the area, while the latter refers to the specific peak.

Chapter 4

1 Not that there was anything wrong with the first—but this second version was more specific in areas particularly

relevant to their changing circumstances.
2 J. Douma, *The Ten Commandments: Manual for the Christian Life* (Phillipsburg, NJ: P&R, 1996), p. 352.
3 There has been a long-running debate about whether the fifth commandment rightly belongs with the first four or the last five. Parents, it is argued, represent God and mediate his authority in the home. The five–five split does seem the more natural one. Whichever way you want to split them, there is no clear biblical reason to think that they were split in that way between the two stones. It may well be that the two stones were identical copies—which some argue was common practice when a covenant was entered into. The Bible doesn't give us enough information to be sure.

Chapter 5
1 'Free, undeserved favour' is a good working definition of grace.

2 It is unclear whether the reference to hornets in v. 20 is supposed to be taken literally or metaphorically. The meaning of the Hebrew word is debated too. The way in which the Lord will deal with their enemies is not as important as the fact that he will.

Chapter 9
1 Sometimes called his will of decree (see Eph. 1).

Chapter 10
1 Linguists refer to it as an 'emphatic negative'.
2 'Funny Insurance Claims Form Gaffes' at businessballs.com; accessed July 2015.
3 'About This Web Site', Acacia John Bunyan Online Library, acacia.pair.com/Acacia.John.Bunyan/About.This.Site.html; accessed 10 June 2015; also 'How to Slay Sin Part 3', 24 February 2011, Grace to You, www.gty.org.uk/blog/2/2011.

Chapter 11
1 This is the Hebrew word *chesed*.

2 Sheol was considered the place of the dead, sometimes depicted as the lowest place in creation, and closely equates to our abstract concept of 'the grave'.

Chapter 12

1 The Hebrew is difficult in verse 2 and could be speaking of the Lord leaving the heavenly hosts to come down, or of leading the hosts of Israel. The context, and especially the use of 'holy ones' again in verse 3, suggests the latter.

2 These blessings are framed as prayers, but the tribes could be sure that Moses' prayers were uttered under the inspiration of the Spirit of God and would be answered. The opening verse of the chapter makes it clear that these prayers amounted to blessings.

3 The NIV opts for a more positive translation here, but one not supported by later events (see 2 Kings 10:33).

4 Who is being referred to in the second half of verse 8 isn't entirely clear. It seems most likely, given the accounts in Exodus and Numbers, that Moses, having addressed the Lord in the first half of the verse, is now addressing the people. This kind of sudden switch is not uncommon in Hebrew poetry. The alternative forces us to read it as the Lord himself who 'tests' and 'quarrels' with Moses and Aaron. While the people were certainly disobedient and then punished, I don't think the words 'test' and 'quarrel' fit the context well, so I prefer the interpretation I have given.

5 The NIV reading, while painting an appealing picture of a place of safety with the Lord carrying the tribe on his back, doesn't seem to be supported by the Hebrew. Another possible translation is 'dwells between his weapons', suggesting the Lord's enabling in battle.

6 Verse 18 is probably proverbial, like the phrase 'comings and goings'—see also Ps. 121:8.

7 Simeon is omitted from the tribes here, presumably because they were to lose their identity and ultimately be swallowed up by Judah, as prophesied in Gen. 49:7.

8 The name 'Jesus' is a translation of the name 'Joshua' and is essentially the same word.

Further resources

Brown, Paul E., *Exploring the Bible: Deuteronomy* (Leominster: Day One, 2008)

Brown, Raymond, *The Message of Deuteronomy* (Leicester: IVP, 1993)

Harman, Allan, *Deuteronomy: The Commands of a Covenant God* (Focus on the Bible; Fearn: Christian Focus, 2001)

Millar, J. Gary, *Now Choose Life: Theology and Ethics in Deuteronomy* (Leicester: Apollos, 1998)

Stewart, Andrew, *Deuteronomy: God's Treasured Possession* (Darlington: Evangelical Press, 2013)

Wright, Christopher, *Deuteronomy* (New International Biblical Commentary; Peabody, MA: Hendrickson / Carlisle: Paternoster, 1996)

About Day One:

Day One's threefold commitment:

- To be faithful to the Bible, God's inerrant, infallible Word;
- To be relevant to our modern generation;
- To be excellent in our publication standards.

I continue to be thankful for the publications of Day One. They are biblical; they have sound theology; and they are relative to the issues at hand. The material is condensed and manageable while, at the same time, being complete—a challenging balance to find. We are happy in our ministry to make use of these excellent publications.

JOHN MACARTHUR, PASTOR-TEACHER, GRACE COMMUNITY CHURCH, CALIFORNIA

It is a great encouragement to see Day One making such excellent progress. Their publications are always biblical, accessible and attractively produced, with no compromise on quality. Long may their progress continue and increase!

JOHN BLANCHARD, AUTHOR, EVANGELIST AND APOLOGIST

Visit our websites for more information and to request a free catalogue of our books.

www.dayone.co.uk